TOMMY

A LIFE AT THE SOCCER FACTORY

TOMMY TYNAN
WITH RICHARD COWDERY

BUD BOOKS

First published by Bud Books, in 1990.

BUD BOOKS
19 Poplar Close
Plympton
Devon
PL7 3GE

ISBN: 0 9516350 0 X

Cover design and layout by Nick Carney.
Printed and typeset in Devon by the Design & Print Workshop Ltd, Barn Close, Langage Industrial Estate, Plymouth, Devon.

For Elaine, Tammy, Keeley, Jordanna and Thomas junior

If a man has a talent and cannot use it,
He has failed.
If he has a talent and he uses only half of it,
He has partly failed.
If he has a talent and learns somehow to use the whole of it,
He has gloriously succeeded,
And won a satisfaction and triumph few men ever know.

THOMAS WOLFE

CONTENTS

Preface

Introduction

1: An End and New Beginnings

A total misunderstanding
Feeling the benefit
A large soft spot

2: Under New Management

Like a holiday camp
A man of few words
Style wars

3: The Be All and End All

Quantity, not quality
A totally different life

A dream come true
The right decision

4: Showdown in Sheffield

Not worth it
The worst of times
A kick up the backside

5: A Routine Life

The soccer factory
Taking the edge off
Like a never-ending party
Indifferent welcomes
Two wasted days

6: On a Pedestal

Restrictive practices
Life in a goldfish bowl
Post-match traumas
Joe Who?
Noises off
Giving something back

7: Money, That's the Problem

Budgeting for success
Shrinking assets
Super Leagues and megabucks

8: Self-Preservation

Written off
Grounds for concern

9: Return Ticket to Plymouth

A bit of a hero
Second time around
Leading from the front

10: Scenes Behind the Scene

Myth and motivation
Squaring up
Aggression and intimidation

11: Success

From Home Park to Villa Park
European excursions
On the up and up

12: All in the Family

A woman's touch
Playing away
Master plumber
Me and mine
A turning point

13: Stimulating Times

A legend in his own drinking up time
Safety in numbers
Being dealt a blow
The perfect image
Tommy Argyle

14: Racism and Hooliganism

Mixing politics and sport
Fighting talk
Under whose influence?

15: Professionalism

Responding to orders
Staying on and sendings-off
Double standards
Getting away with it
Professionals for professionals
Missing, presumed surplus to requirements

16: The Future

Managing by myself
A little application
Finishing thoughts

17: The Best of Teams

Argyle elite
By my side
A dream team
Bar none

Appendices

Statistical breakdown
Acknowledgements

PREFACE

OCTOBER 18, 1975. Unnoticed by the majority of football followers, a Liverpool teenager on loan to Swansea City scores the Welsh club's only goal in a 2-1 defeat away to Doncaster Rovers.

Few people at the Belle Vue Ground that afternoon, let alone Tommy Tynan himself, could have realised they were witnessing the start of a goalscoring career as enduring as any in the modern game.

Tynan has barely stopped scoring since. In 704 senior professional games to the end of the 1989/90 season, he has found the net 291 times. From Plymouth Argyle to Carlisle United, from Newport County to Ipswich Town, there is hardly a Football League club which has succeeded in quenching his lust for goals.

He began his professional career in 1972 at Anfield - on whose terraces he had previously stood to watch his still beloved Liverpool - in unlikely circumstances, winning through to the final stages of the Liverpool Echo newspaper's Search for a Star contest.

But, despite impressing with two goals during a six-match loan period at Swansea, he failed to break into Liverpool's star-studded first-team and, after three years, eventually decided to sever his Merseyside ties and start afresh at Sheffield Wednesday.

He played 91 times in two seasons at Hillsborough, scoring 31 goals and winning instant popularity with the supporters - one of whom, Elaine, he courted and later married - but not with Jack Charlton, who sold him to Lincoln City in 1978.

The move to Sincil Bank proved to be a disaster. So much so that he came close to abandoning the game altogether. But after just nine games, one goal, and another long period of reserve team soccer, Newport County manager Len Ashurst - who had signed him for Sheffield Wednesday - rescued him.

Happy once again, he scored 86 goals in 229 games during 4 1/2 years at Somerton Park and, alongside John Aldridge, played a large part in the Welsh club's 1980/81 European Cup-Winners Cup success.

He left Newport to sign for Bobby Moncur at Plymouth Argyle before the beginning of the 1983/84 season and, though Moncur left soon afterwards, Tynan, now approaching his peak, stayed to score 52 goals in two personally rewarding seasons. In 1983/84, he spearheaded the attack for Argyle as the club reached the FA Cup semi-final and the following season he won a Golden Boot for being the Third Division's leading scorer, with 31 league goals, as well as the supporters' Player-of-the-Year award.

That feat immediately preceded a move to Rotherham United, for who he scored 17 goals in 39 games of the 1985/86 season, at the end of which, after falling out with manager Norman Hunter, he found himself back at Plymouth on loan.

In nine games, he scored ten goals which sealed not only Argyle's promotion to the Second Division but also his status as a folk idol with the Westcountry public.

He returned to Home Park permanently the following year and continued to find the net with pleasing regularity. By the time he was given a free transfer by manager David Kemp at the end of the 1989/90 season, he had been leading scorer for the club for six of the past seven seasons, won the Player-of-the-Year award twice more and had missed just five games in four years.

The door that Kemp closed preceded the opening of another by Torquay United manager Dave Smith who knew and respected Tynan from their days together at Plymouth. Smith persuaded his former striker to link up with him and begin the second phase of his career in the national game, as player-coach at Plainmoor.

Tynan remains deeply attached to the Westcountry, where he lives in Plymouth with Elaine and their four children Tammy, 18, Keeley, 16, Jordanna, 9, and Thomas junior, 4.

The idea for this book came about while I was working with Tynan on a series of articles for the Western Morning News about his life as a professional footballer. After writing five full-page articles, the surface had barely been scratched. There still seemed so more to tell.

What follows is not, nor was ever intended to be, a tale of glitz and glamour. Life at the lower end of the Football League is not chock-full of those qualities.

It can be, and often is, bitchy and boring with occasional moments of intense personal satisfaction. Just like any other job. Tynan and his Plymouth colleagues sometimes referred to the routine times as "another day in the soccer factory" hence the subtitle of the book.

Hopefully, it presents an accurate day-in, day-out reflection of how a journeyman footballer who, despite his prodigiousness, never played in the First Division, but who has made a living from his talents.

The words are all Tynan's, though I confess I may have gently directed his stream of unfettered consciousness. It is, simply, his story.

RICHARD COWDERY 1990

INTRODUCTION

FLIP THROUGH the back pages of the newspapers or switch on the television on a Sunday afternoon and you'd be forgiven for forming the impression that footballers lead glamorous lives.

True, but only for the few elite players in the country's select top sides. The clubs are wealthy, their players are paid wages that your average painter and decorator can only dream about, and fame and success happen with some regularity.

But for every Liverpool and Manchester United, there's a dozen clubs like Aldershot, Hartlepool or Carlisle; for every Ian Rush or Bryan Robson, there's a few hundred journeyman professionals you never hear of; and for every international who wipes out his mortgage with a sponsorship deal, there's tens of Third and Fourth Division professionals who have to be careful with their weekly wage-packet.

For the unsung majority, 95 per cent of the time, football is not a glamorous life. It's purely and simply work, and bloody hard work at that. The bulk of professional footballers are not millionaires, and never will be, but most are as devoted as any star name.

This is my story and it is dedicated to my fellow professionals, past and present; to the Second, Third and Fourth Division players I have enjoyed playing with and against.

It is also dedicated, with love, to my wife Elaine, without who I would have had a very different story to tell.

TOMMY TYNAN 1990

1

AN END AND NEW BEGINNINGS

IN AN ideal situation, I would have loved to have finished my playing career at Plymouth Argyle with a benefit match at the end of it for my services to the club. When Ken Brown was Argyle manager, I was 95 per cent certain that I would get another year's contract and be given a benefit match. He agreed to it and said he'd mentioned it to the board of directors who were also pretty happy with the idea as well. Then he was sacked and I was back in no-man's land again.

I waited two or three weeks after David Kemp had been appointed and then went to see him and explained the situation, that my contract was up in the summer. He told me that he'd see how it went but that if I carried on doing the business, scoring goals, he couldn't see any reason why he couldn't give me another 12 months.

He was happy that I was working hard and training hard, but he did say I could have a couple of days-a-week off training if I wanted to and that offer, which was designed to help me, led to an absolutely ludicrous newspaper story which said that I'd been barred from training. The headline - 'Booted out' - and the story seemed to suggest that I was being unfairly treated, which couldn't have been further from the truth. Anyway, I didn't take him up on his offer. I think I've missed just two days' training in the last five years, which isn't bad for an old codger!

Fortunately, colleagues and friends knew it was a joke but I feel sorry for the fans because a lot of them saw the story and took it literally. The club had to field lots of calls from irate people demanding to know why I was being shoved out of the club.

David Kemp probably didn't want to make a decision at that stage because it wasn't clear whether Plymouth would be playing in the Second or Third Division the following year. I often wonder whether he would have kept me if Argyle had been relegated?

However, I knew my time at Argyle had come to an end two weeks before the end of the 1989/90 season when I went to see David Kemp again. It was the Thursday before Argyle's last home game against Watford. The manager had been honest with me all along the line, which I appreciated, and he simply said he was going to need players that were going to benefit the club in the long-term and that I could have the free transfer I was entitled to.

I don't think there was any embarrassment but it must have been quite hard for him because I was the first player who he had to tell in his career as a manager that they were being let go on a free transfer. It's not a nice thing for a manager to have to do, but he's been through it as a player and we both understood the situation.

I could follow his line of thinking. He's still got a bit of experience at the club in players like Rhys Wilmot, Adrian Burrows, John Brimacombe and Kevin Hodges and needs to add a little bit of youth to get a good blend.

A total misunderstanding

I don't think the decision to let me go was 100 per cent his own, though. I think his coach, Alan Gillett had something to do with it, which is fair enough. Managers and coaches are meant to work together. During the five or six weeks before Alan Gillett arrived, I was very sure that I was going to get a new contract. I scored a couple of goals and played quite well, especially away from home, and David Kemp had been okay, even praised me. I think he changed his mind when Alan Gillett came. To back up what I think, Argyle defender Danny Salman told me that David Kemp had nothing but praise for me when he bought him from Millwall. Danny said he couldn't understand it when I was given a free transfer. I think Alan Gillett prefers youth rather than experience and, to be fair, he'll get the best out of the kids with his methods.

After I'd been told I was being released, the situation was that I agreed to play in the Watford game because we weren't safe from relegation, but wanted to be left out of the following week's trip to Bradford if we had avoided the drop by then, although David Kemp wanted me to play in that game as well.

The reason why I was happy not to play was because there has been a young lad at Argyle who has deserved his chance for years but never really got it - Owen Pickard. I told the manager he should take the opportunity to have a look at Owen. He thought that was a good idea but still wanted me to travel as substitute, which I didn't want to do. I thought that was defeating the object of the idea. If I went all the way to Bradford, I wanted to play. He said he'd think about it and when I came in on Friday morning, the day we were due to travel, I found he'd put me down as a non-playing 14th man, which I was aghast at.

It was a total misunderstanding. He'd thought I would want to still be part of the set-up. But it wasn't like that. There was no row, like some people have made out. I can honestly say that David Kemp and I have never had a wrong word with each other. He thought he was doing me a favour and was a little bit baffled that I didn't want to travel. I might have gone along for the ride if the match had been a little closer to home. But Bradford? No thanks.

So my Argyle farewell was the Watford game and, although it hadn't been announced officially, it was one of the worst kept secrets in the Westcountry. The manager had already said that he wasn't going to make any official announcements until the end of the season but most people were aware that I would never play for Argyle again.

I wasn't too sorry that I missed out on expressing my thanks to the fans because of the official secrecy. That's what my benefit game is for. I've always had a good rapport with the Argyle supporters and the benefit game will give me a chance to say thank you to them.

Feeling the benefit

David Kemp has said that he will do anything he can to help ne with my benefit game, which is very good of him. And it is also very good of the Argyle board to grant me a benefit, because they weren't obliged to. The decision was at their discretion.

I have tried to get Liverpool down but they are very busy and, sadly, can't make it. I've got a few other irons in the fire at the time of writing and will be contacting Glasgow Rangers through Phil Boersma, who I know well from my Liverpool days; John Toshack, at Real Madrid, and Manchester United. But, whoever Argyle play and whenever the match is arranged, I hope the fans and I can have an enjoyable night. And an emotional one.

The fans have been terrific. Since I've left Plymouth, the reaction I've had from people when I've been out walking in the city centre has been unbelievable. Everyday, I've had people coming up to me, shaking me by the hand and saying: "Thanks for all you've done for Argyle and hope you do well in your new career." It's been really nice.

I was on the dole for three weeks after I finished at Plymouth. I disliked it intensely but it was a case of having to because I didn't know what was around the corner. I received the grand sum of £18.63! Thankfully, within ten days of being out of work, several different clubs had come in for me. I talked to Chester, Cardiff, Bury, Halifax, Torquay, someone from Malta whose name I can't even remember, and an agent representing clubs in Holland and Japan. Japan tempted me but you're out of the game completely when you're over there and I was also worried about moving the kids.

I spoke to Torquay first, five days before I was due to go on holiday and Len Ashurst, the Cardiff manager, the following day. I hadn't really intended to speak to Len at all but I didn't think it would ever be possible to reach terms with Torquay because what I wanted and what their new chairman, Mike Bateson was offering were poles apart. What I was asking for wasn't extortionate either. All the clubs I heard from agreed my terms except Torquay. I wanted things sorted before I went on holiday so I spoke to Len Ashurst, who was staying in Torbay.

He said yes to whatever I asked for and we parted with me agreeing to sign for Cardiff when I returned from holiday. Torquay came back to me and I told them I had decided to join Cardiff. Then the chairman said that he would match whatever Cardiff were offering, which was strange because we had been so far away from a deal two days previously.

I think Torquay manager Dave Smith had a lot to do with it. In fact, I know he did because Mike Bateson said that he'd learnt a few things about football very quickly thanks to Dave Smith's boot up his backside. Dave Smith wanted me at Torquay and he had predicted to his new chairman what I would ask for before I even spoke to them. He overestimated by £50.

Mike Bateson is a very ambitious chairman, very high-profile, and willing to put his money where his mouth is, which is good for Torquay. The club has been a soccer backwater, run as a Fourth Division club, for too long. Dave Smith and Mike Bateson are determined that it will become a decent professional football club.

Everyone knows Smithy is a little bit eccentric. That's the way he is. But he's good to work for and I know what he requires from me and from his players. We've had a good working relationship before, at Plymouth, and hopefully it will carry on at Plainmoor.

Signing for Torquay meant that I had to let down Len Ashurst badly and that wasn't a very nice thing to have to do because I've got the utmost respect for him. Len wanted me badly. All the clubs I spoke to offered me terms as a player but Cardiff said they'd put me on the playing staff as player-coach. I think that was just to get me as a player. With Dave Smith, I will be a proper coach, not just a coach in name, which is one of the main reasons why Torquay interested me.

The way I'm looking at it is to concentrate mainly on playing for the first 12 months of my contract and do a lot more of the coaching next year. But I don't know exactly how long I will continue playing. I said three years ago that I'd give myself another two years! It simply depends how I feel. I felt absolutely shattered at the end of last season and maybe David Kemp was right to suggest that I took the odd couple of days off training. Perhaps that's what I'll have to at Torquay this year. But you play a lot more games as a Fourth Division side, so there's less time for real hard days' training sessions.

It's a long time since I played in the Fourth Division and I haven't seen too many matches at that level, but people I've spoken to have said the standard isn't that high. You've got one or two good sides and the rest are all of the same standard. The work-rate is harder because players lack the skill.

A large soft spot

It'll be a little bit strange not starting a new season wearing a green shirt and I'm sad that I won't be doing that. It's been six years of my life and I would have liked to have made it seven before I called it a day. But I'm a professional and scoring goals for Torquay is my living now. That and coaching, which I'm really looking forward to.

I don't think being both a player and a coach will be compromising, because I've done enough in the game to earn respect from players. Also I don't suppose I'll be socialising with the players too much, so they won't feel like I'm spying on them when they go out. But, whether I get changed with the manager or with the rest of the lads, we're all fighting for the same ends. Points and bonuses. It's up to everyone to get on with it.

I think there might be some difficulty. Other players have told me that there is a certain amount of strain when you, as coach, are critical of players that you're playing alongside. I'm also going to have to overcome the temptation to coach while I'm playing. The trick is to do the training at the training ground and the playing on the pitch. I've got to forget about coaching when I'm on the field and, knowing myself, that won't be very hard. I've been bought primarily as a player for the next year because Torquay want the goals that will take them to the Third Division.

Unfortunately, I doubt whether I can build such a large rapport with the Torquay fans as I managed at Argyle. I didn't have an instant love affair with the Plymouth public, more of a slow-burning romance, and I won't have that much time at Plainmoor. It would be nice to hit it off straight away, but unlikely. I've got to go in and score a few goals and if I don't I've got to take the stick that's coming. I'll get people having a go if I have a bad time but I've had that before and come through it. It won't be a new experience.

Of course, I'll always have a very large soft spot for Plymouth Argyle. Torquay are playing their home matches on a Friday evening now, so I'll probably go up the road to keep an eye on Plymouth on Saturday afternoons and see what's going on. Maybe I'll even try and poach a few players!

One player does not make a team and I'm not blowing my own trumpet, but it is going to be difficult for Argyle to replace me. When they do find someone who scores 25 goals-a-season, it will be a case of "The king is dead, long live the king". But whoever replaces me will have a hard job and my message to Argyle supporters is not to be critical of anyone who plays in my old position. Especially someone like Owen Pickard, who is a still a young lad. Don't expect too much too quickly.

Plymouth fans are very critical because they haven't had a great deal of success and they want something to cheer about so desperately. But they will have to be patient with the younger players, especially Owen. He has proved he can score goals but it will take time for him to establish himself at Football League level.

You cannot change history and I'm in the club record books for being Argyle's leading post-war goalscorer, scoring 100 league goals in the shortest time, and winning the Player-of-the-Year award three times. I've done it. It's recorded in black-and-white and someone'll have to work very hard and do very well to erase my name.

I'm not bitter about anything, me, especially in football. All good things come to an end and hopefully Plymouth will go onto better things. I think they are long overdue a place in the First Division and next season could be*the* season. I'm hoping that Argyle and Torquay achieve a Westcountry promotion double next May.

2

UNDER NEW MANAGEMENT

MY FINAL season at Plymouth Argyle last year was not one of the best, either for me personally or for the club. After a bright start, the side was always struggling to string together some decent results.

I scored 18 goals, which was not a bad total but not a tremendous one by my own standards, had the captaincy taken away from me and was dropped - by Ken Brown - for only the second time in all my seasons at Home Park.

Because of our poor form, which at one stage looked likely to lead to relegation to the Third Division, Ken Brown was sacked two-thirds of the way through the season.

I thought his sacking was handled very shabbily by the club. For a start, the Plymouth players were the last to know and, to be honest, players should be among the first to know when directors have sacked the manager. They are the ones most affected. The press were told before we were and that was disgraceful.

Graham Little, the club secretary, came down to the dressing room, where we'd been waiting for about half-an-hour after finishing training, and said the directors wanted to see Nicky Marker, who had taken over from me as team captain.

Nicky went to the board-room and was apparently asked by the directors if he was the club captain. When he said he wasn't, they said that he would do anyway and told him that the manager had been sacked. He then relayed the news to the rest of the lads.

I think the lads would have respected the board more if the chairman had come to see the players and told them the situation, rather than relay the news through the team captain. I felt it needed someone in authority to stamp himself on the situation. The board had sacked the manager, so why couldn't the directors tell us that themselves? Why did they have to go through a second party?

I couldn't believe my ears when Ken Brown came to the dressing room to confirm and explain what we had been told through Nicky. The directors had just sacked a manager whose decisions had at least partly contributed to our dire position but then taken his advice on who to appoint as his replacement. I think that was crazy and that is no way a reflection on the ability of John Gregory, who was Ken Brown's recommendation to the board.

Although we were officially the last to know about the sacking, we had realised something was up. We'd had another bad result against Wolves on Saturday afternoon and on Monday morning all the directors were at the club. When you arrive for training and you see all the Jags and BMWs, you don't need to be psychic to draw your conclusions.

We knew something was going on and one look at Ken Brown's son Kenny, the Plymouth right-back, confirmed what was going through our minds. Kenny came in for training at 9.30 am and did not say a word for 1 1/2 hours. He was very subdued. He admitted afterwards that he knew about the sacking but that his dad had asked him not to say anything to anyone about it. It must have been very difficult for him.

The difficulties didn't end with the sacking either. The fans were still openly critical of Ken Brown long after he was sacked, which doesn't surprise me, but it must have been hard for Kenny because those remarks are going to hurt you if you've got any feelings for your father.

But I think Kenny's proved his maturity and professionalism by playing through it. He's stayed at Argyle and held down his place in the side, which should put paid to the belief that he was only in the team because his father was the manager. It wasn't just some of the fans who thought that, either. Certain Plymouth players believe that young Jason Rowbotham is a better right-back than Kenny.

I think Kenny became a better player as last season progressed and that he'll continue to get better with experience. He's still quite young and learning all the time.

Like a holiday camp

In a way, Ken Brown's sacking was very sad. I don't think there was one person at the club who wished him any harm or was pleased that he went, because he was such a nice man.

Probably the major factor that went against him was that he wasn't hard enough when the chips were down. He liked things to be loose and relaxed. There was a generally jovial atmosphere at Home Park and everyone enjoyed their training. But it was a little too lacking in seriousness really.

I would say that 95 per cent of the players at the club were sorry to see him go. Everyone felt they'd let him down, especially the players that he'd bought. I loved the way he wanted his players to play but he was a little too soft on us. The whole situation, the whole mood of the club, was too lax. Some people have said it was like a holiday camp and that's a fair comment.

I think he should have got more of a grip on things when we weren't doing well, told everyone to buckle their belts in, and tried a few new routines in training to shake everyone up a bit. But he let it go on too long and, in the end, I'm afraid the inevitable happened.

At the end of the day, we, the players, let him down. He put his faith in the players he had and we didn't get the results. We knew we were letting him down. Once, after yet another defeat, we all sat down in the dressing room and said: "We have got to get results or this man is out of a job." We didn't get the results and the board sacked him. It's a simple equation really. Bad results don't get players the sack; they get managers the sack.

Who can tell whether Ken Brown would have turned things around if he'd been left in charge for another few weeks? Whether we might have got the results to get us out of the mire? But it didn't happen that way. It's a shame though, that a fellow of his calibre and his knowledge had to go the way he did.

Personally, I think the directors might have been a little bit hasty, but if you look at the situation from their point of view, there were still 19 games to go before the end of the season and whoever came in still had a half-decent chance of keeping the club in the Second Division. Having said that, I didn't expect Ken Brown to be sacked after the Wolves game. I thought he still had another couple of weeks to effect a cure.

Ken Brown, to his credit, did not appear too bitter when he said his goodbyes to the players who had effectively let him down. He addressed the players in the dressing room, saying that he'd been released by the club and that he'd advised the board that John Gregory was the man for the job.

I was amazed that the board agreed to that and I also believe that John Gregory's appointment was the main reason why Martin Harvey, the club coach, resigned a few days later. To be looked over in favour of a man who'd only been at the club for two or three weeks must have been very hard for him to accept.

I felt the directors should have let Martin Harvey take temporary charge, which is what would normally happen at most clubs: control automatically passes to the second-in-command when the manager is sacked. Martin Harvey was the first-team coach and natural successor, and when he was passed over in favour of John Gregory I think he felt the board had dealt him a huge slap in the face.

Martin Harvey, and Malcolm Musgrove, the physiotherapist and trainer, didn't take as much of the training while John Gregory was temporary manager as they had done during Ken Brown's time. John Gregory took complete control of everything. Martin Harvey said that he felt like a glorified ball-boy in training and a lot of the lads didn't like the fact that he had apparently been pushed aside. He was very well respected by the players.

John Gregory's appointment was a surprise but not a total shock. Most of Plymouth's followers, not to mention the players, believed that he'd been bought by Ken Brown not as a player, but as a coach or a future team manager - with Ken Brown moving up to general manager. I thought that might have happened at the end of the season and I think it might have worked.

In the short time he was at Plymouth, John Gregory proved he enjoyed playing the sort of fluent, creative football that players enjoy playing, and the lads certainly enjoyed his training sessions. His routines were short and sharp, and designed to get the best out of you. He worked us very hard, but the sessions were always enjoyable.

John Gregory was in a very difficult situation. He was effectively manager of the club, but he didn't know how long that situation was going to last. When he first spoke to the players, he simply said that all the board had asked him to do was to pick a side for the next match. But within ten days he had completely changed the club. He stopped drinks on the coach, for instance, and banned players from playing golf two days before a match.

He brought in his own rules which, to some extent, he had to do to create a favourable impression. After all, he must have hoped he could land the job on a full-time basis, and I think that might have happened if the results had picked up.

I'm not saying they were the wrong things to do, just that they were the actions of a manager in total control, not someone who was going to pick a side for the next match. A lot of the players didn't like that situation.

But although he brought new rules in, he never fined a player. There was one time when two players deliberately missed a walk we were all supposed to go on, but he took no action when he found out about it, except confront the absentees. There were a couple of other occasions when players were late for training, but they weren't fined either. He could pick the side, introduce new rules, take the training, even sign players if he'd wanted to, but not fine players. I found the situation strange, to say the least.

A man of few words

The press were told about Ken Brown's sacking before the players, and the same situation occurred with the appointment of David Kemp as his successor. The first I knew about David Kemp's appointment was when I read about it in the paper that evening and saw it on television a bit later. We should have been told first. What would it have taken? Twenty or so phone calls from the club to their staff to say that the new manager had been appointed.

It infuriates me how players are sometimes taken for granted. Managers and players are expected to be professional in everything they do and they get slaughtered - quite rightly - when they act unprofessionally. But the board of directors can act very amateurishly and no-one says anything.

Having said that, their appointment saved the club from relegation to the Third Division. To be honest though, the directors didn't make too many right decisions during my time at Plymouth. They must bear some responsibility for Plymouth Argyle's failure under Ken Brown. They appointed him and he let them down, so they sacked him. They appointed the wrong man. They believed in him, the same way that Ken Brown believed in his players. We didn't do it for him, so he was sacked; he didn't do it for them, yet they came out of the affair unscathed. It's a little cock-eyed.

Whoever the board appoints, they will think they have made the right decision. Only success or failure will prove them right or wrong.

David Kemp was a man of few words on his first day. He got us together and said: "You're near the bottom of the table; things need to be changed and I'm going to make changes" and took us out for a half-hour eight-a-side game before picking the team for the following day's game.

He changed our style of football from Ken Brown's patient build-ups to what he calls "no-risk" football, which basically means not playing at all in your own half of the field, only in the opposition's half, getting the ball up to your front men as quickly as possible, knocking balls in behind their defence and trying to create as much havoc as possible. That was the way he wanted to play on day one, and that's the way he's played ever since.

One thing which he did introduce, which we didn't have under Ken Brown and which I think was needed, was a pattern of play. It's simply playing to a system in which players are expected to be in certain positions and certain areas of the field at certain times, for the benefit of the whole side and for general organisation.

Ken Brown used to tell the players simply to go out and play football. That's all very well, but not even Liverpool do that and they are the best team in the country. We needed a pattern of play because there were some players on the field who didn't know what they were supposed to be doing and where they were supposed to be at certain times. When you talk about discipline on the field, you are talking about being told what you must and mustn't do, and obeying that. Maybe David Kemp has brought back a little bit of Saturday afternoon discipline that was missing under Ken Brown.

David Kemp works very hard on set-pieces, in both attack and defence. When we went through other teams' free-kicks, he would put their team on a board - with a diagram - and list who should be marking who in every situation. That way, there could be no argument about who was supposed to be watching which opponent when he knocked a goal in. It was written on a piece of paper for everyone to see. That's the theory, of course, and it didn't always work, but he's the boss and that's what he wants.

Personally, I've got my reservations about his style. I think the players took it a little too literally at times last season. They'd would just hoof the ball forward anywhere and anyhow, and I don't think that is what he wanted. Teams like Watford and Wimbledon play the long-ball game but they don't just hack the ball anywhere. They hit 40 or 50-yard passes into certain areas of the field for the benefit of their forwards.

Style wars

David Kemp was not an up-and-under merchant when he was a player, he was a footballer. But he's been at Wimbledon, where he's seen average players get success with the system and he believes in it. He believes that the system will work with any 11 players, as long as they adhere to it. When he first came to Plymouth, he told us that he didn't really need to go out and buy new players if the ones that he'd inherited believed in what he was doing. By introducing his pattern of play and only a few new players, he has showed that it can work, too.

Initially, it was difficult for the players to adapt to the new methods. We'd gone from Dave Smith's long-ball style, to Ken Brown's patient style - which took a long time to get right, though probably we never did get it properly right - and then to David Kemp's own particular long-ball style.

It took six or seven games to get right and all that time he didn't really mind us getting beaten if we had tried to carry out his instructions - lifting balls over their back-four to create chances - but he was naturally upset if we hadn't obeyed orders.

He is one of the few managers I have played under who you could talk to and know that he would act on it if what you said registered with him. I mentioned a couple of things to him when we were up in Newcastle which he listened to, obviously thought about and acted on. A lot of managers will not do that, but David Kemp is very receptive and will not take offence or make judgements on you if you talk openly to him.

He's also the only manager I can remember having a drink with the players and supporters after home games. I don't know whether that's because he's only been out of the game as a player for a few years and still finds it difficult to detach himself from that life-style. But I believe it's a great precedent to set. He's quite intense - most managers are and it's his first senior job and he wants desperately to be a success - but he's a great one for having a few drinks after the football's over and, temporar-

-ily, forgetting about it.

If David Kemp finds the sort of players who believe in and can bring out the best from his style of play and if, more importantly, he is given the money to buy those players, I'm sure he'll be successful. There's not many teams in the Second Division that play his way, so it will not be easy to combat next season.

In the air with Budgie: Up against Newcastle goalkeeper John Burridge.

A dig in the ribs: Giving Sunderland captain Gary Bennett the elbow.

Lean times: Shadowed by Mark Morris, of Sheffield United.

Heads I lose: Beaten to the ball by the Blackburn Rovers defence.

Out-foxed: About to lose out against Leicester's Paul Ramsey.

Three on two: Head and shoulders above Ron Futcher of Bradford City.

A kick up the backside: On the receiving end against Bournemouth.

Laying off: Looking for a team-mate against Oxford United.

3

THE BE ALL AND END ALL

FOR ME, football has been the be all and end all of my life for the whole of my life, although I never really thought of it like that in the early part of my career. I've never wanted to do anything else but play football for a living, although I did go through a phase where I wanted to enjoy life too much at the same time as playing football and, as I discovered, the two didn't mix.

Probably because I've been in the game so long, I know what you can get out of it through personal success. The last seven years of my career have been the best, without a doubt. I've looked after myself and I've got more out of life because of that. Everything has been alright financially, my family has always had a good standard of living and never been short of a pound or two. I've got the football right and everything else has come right because of that. When you're doing well, people like you, and, if people like me, I'm happy.

I can honestly say it will be the worst day of my life when I retire from playing. My life has been geared around playing football for the last 18 years and, basically, I love it.

You never really leave football if you become a coach or a manager because you still take part in the daily five-a-sides and are still in training, of sorts. You're still involved. But it would be very hard for me if I have to leave football altogether. In the past, there have been times when I've been almost waiting for it to happen and I not knowing what I will do next. I don't ever want to imagine it again.

Most players think they will go on forever. Your head tells you that you can, but it's the legs which tell you that you can't. Each year it takes you longer and longer to get over games. Nowadays, I get stiffer as the days go by. Age is a crippler. In your mind you can still do it, long after your legs have packed up.

I played in two testimonial matches when I was at Sheffield Wednesday and the atmosphere was superb. One was for Ian Macdonald, a Scottish lad, good player, who had to pack it in because his left knee was totally knackered. Because of the atmosphere - there were about 5,500 people there and he got a standing ovation - and the fact that he knew he wasn't going to play again, he actually cried.

He couldn't play in his own testimonial because of his knee, but he shook hands with both captains, waved to the crowd and walked off, taking the crowd's salute. I looked over at him and he was crying his eyes out.

I didn't appreciate how he felt then, but as I've reached the end of my career I have gradually understood his feelings much better.

At the other end of the scale, there are players who couldn't give a damn. I might be wrong but I always got the impression that Alan Waddle, who I played with at Newport, was never really interested in the game.

Another Newport player, Kevin Moore, a good quick winger with loads of ability, wouldn't go out of his way to watch a match after he'd finished. He was a bit of a loner but a very nice lad for who football seemed merely a means to an end. He didn't need football and was only 27 when he quit and went to live in Blackpool and work for his father, who I think was president of the club. He never really needed to make football his living.

I've known other players who can just play football, go home and switch off. There are players in football who don't want to know about the game, apart from training and playing. They don't watch it on telly, or talk about it or have anything else to do with it.

Ninety per cent of footballers are fans but there are a few like Kevin who, after they've finished playing, won't even go and watch a game. I can honestly say that I'd still go and watch football regularly if I have to quit football or if I'd never made it in the game.

Quantity, not quality

Besides scoring goals, everything I do is incidental. Scoring goals is what I'm paid to do and if I'm not scoring, I'm not earning my money, even if I'm playing well.

I scored 22 goals in one season for Plymouth and heard a radio report say that the reason Plymouth had not made the Second Division play-offs was because Tommy Tynan wasn't scoring enough. I'd just gone seven games without scoring.

If the team is not playing well or not winning, you're very critical and you know where the match has gone wrong, but it's very difficult to remember the whole thing blow-by-blow. A lot of professional footballers will remember what they did or didn't do, not what others have done or haven't done. They are concentrating on their own role.

I tend to look at myself first and ask myself whether I am playing well, then I can think about other aspects of the game.

I remember the goals and where the goals have come from. The goals I like to score are ones that come from good moves which I finish. My finish is a strike at goal, a winger's finish is his cross. They might be the best player in the world but if they beat five players and fail to get the ball across, they haven't finished their job.

I don't score many goals from outside the box because that's not what I'm good at. I'm good inside the box and that's it. I like reaction goals. I'll always remember one at Bradford which I scored from six yards out. The ball came to me from a long way out and I just volleyed it and it flew in. It was one of those which either hits the pigeons or goes straight in.

If you look at the goals I've scored, I would say that 270 out of 290 of them have come from five yards out or nearer. I'm not the type of player that is going to walk round three defenders and plant the ball into the net. I depend on getting service from other people and I've played for some sides where I've got tremendous service. Whether it's a tap-in or a volley or a header, as long as it ends up in the back of the net, that's it.

If you ask me whether I'd rather score one forty-yard screamer or ten tap-ins, it would be ten tap-ins every time. Quantity, not quality, is what my game is all about.

Finishing my playing career in Devon is ideal. It would have been very difficult to have moved from the Westcountry. I've a lot of friends down here, people like me and I like them. Mind you, the final move of my career had to be a financially sound move, not just one to the right club.

A totally different life

You never know what's going to happen in football. You could think you've got the future sorted out then someone could come in with an offer that forces you to reconsider the situation, which is what happened to me in the summer. The player-coach job at Plainmoor suits me down to the ground because it means staying in football, which is what I want to do.

It will be hard coming to terms with the idea of never playing football again, when that situation arises, because I've been in the game since I was 16, close to 19 years.

Some players play the game for 20 years, finish, just forget about it and do nothing else. I'm not like that. I love football and I am very lucky to be able to do the only thing I've ever wanted to do since I was four-years-old. There's not many people that can say that.

I've seen another side of life which has been a good experience but which has also made me grateful to have had the ability to earn a living by playing football.

I worked in a pub in Plymouth one summer and enjoyed it because it was totally different from what I'd been used to. I used to come in at 6 am, do all the cleaning up, change the barrels, stock the shelves, and a little bit of the management side of things. But most of what I did was work behind the bar.

For six weeks, I lived a totally different life and I really enjoyed it. It kept me off the streets and, to be honest, I drank less than I normally would because it can get very busy behind the bar of a pub. The only time you get a chance for a drink is just before closing time and then it's just half-a-lager because you've got to re-stock the shelves after the pub closes.

I also spent one summer in Newport working five days-a-week as a labourer. I enjoyed it, but it also made me realise what hard work it is. The money came in handy as I was only on a basic wage from the club - no win or draw bonuses during the summer - and it also gave me something to do during the week.

I've also worked for a friend of mine who has got his own scrap-metal business. That's even worse than labouring. He taught me how to use an oxyacetylene torch and I'd slice through the scrap metal. That's basically all I did.

So I've got an insight into what people do to work hard for a living. About 90 per cent of people who come and watch football come from the working classes. They work hard for their money and fork out three or four quid for the pleasure of watching you. I know what it's like to work behind a bar or in a scrap-metal yard and I've realised that the rewards for doing that are not very great.

I could have ended up in a scrap-metal yard full-time if I hadn't been lucky enough to be a professional footballer, which is the only real life I've known.

A dream come true

The path towards a life in soccer began back in Liverpool when I was still an enthusiastic schoolboy who discovered quite an unusual way of breaking into the game.

The local evening newspaper, the Liverpool Echo, was running a Search for a Soccer Star promotion, the finals of which were being held in front of Liverpool's coaching staff. So I duly collected the vouchers - six vouchers, from the Monday to the Saturday - filled in the application form, and was invited for a trial in my local area.

After the first trial, I just went on and on. I had about five other trials with FA coaches and the whole thing boiled down to about 20 kids being invited to Melwood, Liverpool's training ground, on a Tuesday night.

They staged two five-a-side games in front of Bill Shankly and his coaches, Bob Paisley, Joe Fagan and Tom Saunders, and afterwards we got to meet them. It was a great night out for the kids and that, in my mind then, was about all. The best thing about it at the time was that you were given a football bag, boots and a certificate saying you'd got through all these trials.

The next night, a fellow called John Bennison, who's now the youth team coach at Anfield, rang and asked me to come down and train at the club once a week. Like I say, I was still at school then. After I'd been training there for a month, they asked me to bring my dad down to the ground.

They told us they wouldn't sign anyone on under the age of 16 but that they wanted to take me on after my next birthday. So I left school, got a part-time job and trained with them twice a week. Then they said: "Come down every day from now on and we'll pay your expenses." They were giving me £30 a week, which was more than I was getting from my job!

It did me a lot of good, getting used to playing and training straight after leaving school, even though it was hard going.

They were as good as their word when I reached 16 and I signed on as an apprentice. It was a dream come true for me. I had been a Liverpool supporter virtually since birth and used to go to every home game with my dad and stand and watch from the Kop.

Suddenly I'd gone from watching to training with the players I used to idolise. Still did idolise. I used to clean the boots of players like Emlyn Hughes, Larry Lloyd and Ray Clemence. I've been to a lot of clubs since where the kids train on their own but at Liverpool they mix them up as much as possible. They warm up together and train together.

The training sessions were an experience in themselves and filled with the legendary incidents that people associate with Liverpool. I always remember Chris Lawler, who was very quiet, very rarely spoke a word. We were playing a five-a-side one day, using markers as posts, and one of Bill Shankly's shots crossed the line about crossbar height. 'Was that in?" asked Shanks. Chris replied: "No boss" and Shanks came straight back: " Bloody hell, that's the first thing you've said for three months...and it's a lie!" Typical Shankly.

Shanks always used to play in the five-a-sides and he never missed a penalty. It happened like this. The games were always staff versus apprentices and if the staff got a penalty, Shanks would make you mark the goal out. As you turned your back, he simply banged the ball past you. The worse thing that could happen to you if you were an apprentice would be to be drafted onto the staff side because they would simply make you run about all the time.

I was lucky in my first year with the Liverpool youth team. We reached the final of the FA Youth Cup where we got beaten 5-2 by Aston Villa, and I got quite a few goals on the way.

I was playing in the A team as soon as I signed as an apprentice. I scored on my debut but I couldn't get in again and I was relegated to the B team for the next match. It was like that at Liverpool; the reserve team was often made up of eleven professionals and they even had a C team made up of non-contract players who played for other clubs, and schoolboys. It was an unbelievable set-up.

The right decision

I signed professional when I was 17. In the first game of one season I scored five goals for the A team. I scored another eight in the next four games but I still couldn't get in the reserves because it contained people like Alec Lindsay, Phil Boersma, Ian Callaghan, Steve Heighway, even John Toshack.

After a while kicking my heels, waiting for a chance, the manager, Bob Paisley said to me: "Do you want to go to Swansea for a month? Purely on loan. We don't want you to sign for them permanently." I went for six games and scored a couple of goals even though it was a bit harder physically than I'd been used to. But there was never any question of me leaving Liverpool at that stage. I used Swansea to gain experience and they used me to fill a gap in their forward line.

I came back for the rest of the season and then spent the following summer in America on loan at Dallas, which was quite a good experience. More of a holiday than playing football. I was a bit disillusioned with reserve team football when I came back, though.

Most professionals will tell you, whether they play in the First Division or the Fourth, that first-team football is what it's all about - it's the only way to get a mention. I'd seen too many people at Liverpool who were 26 or 27 and who had made a reasonable living playing hundreds of games in the reserves, but who had nothing to show for it.

I returned from America and Bob Paisley offered me a new two-year contract. I said: "I want first-team football and you can't guarantee me that." He told me I might be able to break through in the next couple of years, but by then I would have been 23. I wanted away.

Then Sheffield Wednesday, who were then in the Third Division, came in for me. I spoke to them and quickly agreed terms. When I arrived there I met a fellow called Chris Turner, a 17-year-old in his first year as a professional, who had already played about fifty first-team games. That brought it home to me and I knew that I had made the right decision to leave Liverpool.

4

SHOWDOWN IN SHEFFIELD

LEN ASHURST was the manager at Sheffield Wednesday when they bought me from Liverpool. I scored 14 Third Division goals in my first year at Hillsborough and the following year, during which Len was replaced by Jack Charlton, I upped that to 21 even though we struggled a little bit.

Things were initially okay after Jack took over but then, suddenly, we didn't see eye-to-eye over certain things and we had a few ups and downs which eventually resulted in me leaving Hillsborough.

A lot of people still think that Jack Charlton and I clashed over our respective, different, views on football. It was nothing to do with football. Jack Charlton did something to me which I thought was totally out of order because it was nothing at all to do with him.

He tried to rule my personal life and tell me what to do off the field as well as on it. I was 23, old enough to know my own mind and, although I might have been out of order on a couple of occasions, I don't agree with the way he interfered in my personal life.

This is essentially what happened. Wednesday were on their way back from a midweek game at Peterborough, where we'd lost 2-1, and Jack wasn't very happy with our performance. He told everyone that they couldn't go out when we returned to Sheffield. Although it was a Tuesday night, when we would normally have been allowed out for a drink or whatever, he said he didn't want anybody out on the town. I told him I'd arranged to meet my girlfriend, Elaine, at the night-club where she was working. He said that was fair enough as long as I didn't stay out.

So I went to meet Elaine and told her: "I can't stay. We're not allowed out. I've got to go straight away." She said that she'd meet me at my place after she'd finished. Elaine finished at the night-club, picked me up and I went back to her place. We weren't in for training the next day.

At the time, I was living in digs at the home of with another Wednesday player, a fellow called Hughie Dowd. Hughie told me next day that Jack Charlton and the Wednesday trainer, Tony Toms, had called at his house at about 1 am. Hughie said: "You're for it. The manager turned up with Tony Toms last night, asking where you were."

So when I came in on Thursday morning Jack asked me where I had been on Tuesday night. I told him I was at my girlfriend's house and the whole story came out. After that we didn't see eye-to-eye because I thought he was trying to run my private life.

He still didn't believe me. He said: "You went out." I said: "I didn't. I went back, told my girlfriend I couldn't stay, she picked me up after work and we went back to her place." He said: "I went to Dowdie's and you weren't there." I said: "I know I wasn't. Where does it matter where I sleep, at my digs or at my girlfriend's? It was a Tuesday night, we weren't in next day, what's it got to do with you where I sleep? I'm not breaking any rules."

Then I went through a stage when I was scoring quite a few goals. We finished eighth from bottom in the Third Division, I scored 21 goals and was Player-of-the-Year, and he was still trying to rule my life. While he was doing that, I was going the other way. Instead of just saying: "Alright, you might be right" or whatever, I just totally blanked him because he was trying to tell me I shouldn't be going out with Elaine. I don't think he liked the idea of her working in a night-club

I just told him: "She's my girlfriend. I'm going out with her." He would say that because of who I was I could have who I wanted. I said:

"Fair enough, but I've been through all that when I was younger." In Sheffield there was about three women to every man and it was no problem to pull if you were half-decent looking and dressed well.

I don't want to sound big-headed about it but, because I was playing for Sheffield Wednesday and was their leading goal-scorer, I could get who I wanted. There were loads of women about. But I went out with Elaine and he tried to tell me I shouldn't go out with her.

I would tell Jack: "If I'm not doing it on the field, fair enough, but don't interfere with my personal life." In the pre-season, I moved in with Elaine but Jack said he wanted me to move in with him because I was about half-a-stone overweight and he wanted to put me on a diet. I told him I'd lose that in pre-season training, which was always quite hard at Sheffield Wednesday.

But the affair between me and him blew up because of what he was trying to do outside of the football. Most managers give you advice, which is fair enough, but what he tried to do was simply not on.

I've got a feeling he had made up his mind that he was going to sell me when he first came to Hillsborough because he didn't like big stars and I was the Sheffield star, if you like, because I was scoring goals. I don't think he liked that.

After the incident over Elaine, he went to another extreme. He said: "Alright, you've made your choice" and started playing me up front on my own at the beginning of his second season, despite the fact that the previous season's style had seen me score more than 20 goals.

It soon became obvious that the new way wasn't working. He brought me off four games in succession when, personally, I thought I'd been working hard.

I went into his office and told him I couldn't play the way he was asking me to play, that I needed someone big up front with me. He was playing five across the midfield and I told him that I needed a big target-man if he was going to use that sort of system. I told him I couldn't carry on the way things were going and he said: "Either you play this way or not at all." I said: "I'll go on the list." Eventually, he agreed to let me go.

People have told me since that he subsequently put off three sides from signing me and in the end I probably signed for the wrong club, Lincoln City, just to get away. At the time, I thought it was the only way out for me and I made the wrong decision. But I believe I went to the club he wanted me to go to. He probably wanted me out anyway, but a lot of people in Sheffield thought he was wrong to let me go.

He bought a big lad called Andy McCulloch not long after he sold me to Lincoln, which annoyed me because I'd been crying out for a big lad to play off.

It's funny; after I left the club, he was the nicest fellow you could wish to meet. I must have seen him three or four times soon after I left Wednesday. Once when he came to watch Newport he made a point of asking how I was doing. It still baffles me to this day why he couldn't be like that when I was in his side.

All I can put it down to is that he didn't really want me in the Wednesday set-up, but, to be honest, I would rather he'd have said: "I don't think you're the type of player for me, I'll give you a move" than have all the unpleasant feelings. No-one should be able to tell you who your girlfriend should be.

Apparently he's mellowed a little bit now, but at the time I saw red. She was the girlfriend I'd picked, not him. And, alright, he might have been right saying I could do this and that, but I'd made my mind up and I think I've been proved right because I'm still with her and we're married now.

When I later went to Rotherham, the manager Norman Hunter, who had been a playing colleague of Jack's at Leeds United, told me that Jack was out every Thursday night when he was a player, chatting up the birds, although he'd always leave before midnight. He had been like I was, and then was trying to stop me doing the same things that he'd apparently been doing. Maybe he'd learnt from it and was trying to tell me what he had learned.

Maybe I needed sorting out, although I thought I was going along all right. When I moved in with Elaine he repeated that I could have got any bird I wanted if I put my mind to it and pointed out that she'd been married before and had two kids. I said: "So what? I've made up my mind and that's it." I don't think he could understand that and he didn't like the situation, maybe, as I say, because she was working in a night-club.

Jack's not a bad coach but he's got certain ideas about what players should do that don't tally with players ideas of what they should do. Maybe he's been through it and seen the pitfalls, but at the time I didn't agree with him and that's one of the reasons, the main reason, why I left Sheffield Wednesday. I know Elaine got very bitter about it and gave Jack a bit of a verbal over what happened because she didn't want to leave Sheffield, which is her home town.

Not worth it

Apart from the personal side of things, we had some good times. Soon after he came to Wednesday, we went to his mother's farm near Middlesbrough, on a sort of get-to-know-you exercise. Six of us stayed there and six of us somewhere nearby. We were at the farm for four days and it was absolutely brilliant.

Jack's exactly the way people have painted him, a country squire type - he took us shooting and everything. His mother was phenomenal, she must have been a saint. She looked after the six of us tremendously and the food she gave us was unbelievable. I can guarantee you have never seen food in your life like she used to serve up for us - steaks, Yorkshire puddings as big as plates, good home cooking.

One or two things stupid little things happened during those four days that got reported in the local newspaper. Sixteen professionals hit this little village and the place ran out of lager for some reason. It must have been coincidence! There was nothing else to do for entertainment but have a few drinks.

We went to one place and were allowed to stay behind after closing time. Most of us were drunk by the time we emerged and a few wanted to go to the toilet. Unfortunately, we were in this strange village in the middle of the night having a pee in the pitch dark, totally oblivious to the fact that we were peeing on this highly-regarded war memorial. There were a few glasses smashed too, all the result of accidents, nothing deliberate.

Next day, Jack pulled us up after breakfast and asked what had happened. It was probably a little too boisterous for a small village and it all got in the local paper, which he understandably wasn't too happy about.

We were out every night. He even took us down to the pub himself some nights and bought us a few drinks. He made judgements about certain players from those few days away - what sort of personalities they were, who liked a drink, that sort of thing. I think that was wrong because we were relaxing, our guard was down.

Jack Charlton is one of those people who has been extremely successful, has gone right to the heights as a player and a manager. He can't be short of a bob or two but I found trying to get money out of him was like trying to get blood out of a stone. He'd say things like: "You shouldn't be on this money, you're not worth it." I thought: "Well you've made a great living out of it."

He was a decent coach, you can't argue with that. He always gave the impression that he'd like to be one of the lads and it must have been hard for him to adjust to management, especially early in his career.

At Middlesbrough, as well as Sheffield, he didn't have any big stars, just quite a few very good players who got on well with each other. He didn't like people who were outspoken, which I've always been, probably wrongly. His training was good, though. He liked his warm-ups and loved a practice match.

The worst of times

The move to Lincoln proved to be disastrous. Their manager, Willie Bell went off to America to become an evangelist a few days after I signed for them: Colin Murphy came in to replace him and just didn't want to play me. I didn't like him at all and he had the same feelings for me.

Cup and my career took off again. But Lincoln was an important point in my life. I wouldn't be in the game now if I hadn't had the experience at Lincoln.

Still, the following year wasn't one of my better seasons. Len Ashurst went through a phase where he thought I needed a kick up the backside and he would administer that by leaving me out every now and again. He'd had that philosophy ever since we'd been together at Wednesday.

Then he played me in midfield and, before the next season, he told me he'd like me to play there permanently. I said I'd give it a go, had a good pre-season and he promptly left me out for the first game. Then he bought Alan Waddle and Jeff Johnson and, although no-one could have foreseen it at that time, that's what started Newport on the road to ruin.

Newport bought Waddle from Swansea for £80,000 on an eighteen-month contract, gave him a big signing-on fee, and Johnson for £60,000 from Sheffield Wednesday, where he'd been going through as similar situation with Jack Charlton that I had. They appeared to be sound investments at the time. Len is a good judge of a player.

But twelve months later Waddle left on a free transfer and Johnson for just £8,000. For a small club to lose that amount of money was disastrous. After that, they had to sell players simply to keep afloat and eventually even that didn't prevent the players' cheques from bouncing all over the place as the club continued on the downward spiral.

The following season after my spell in midfield, the new manager Colin Addison played me up front all the way through, first with Dave Gwyther and then John Aldridge, with who I had a great, but brief, playing relationship.

Newport was a lovely little club, the people were tremendous, but things happened behind the scenes that you didn't hear about at the time. Money went out of the window left, right and centre and they owed taxes. Eventually I moved to Plymouth, Steve Lowndes went to Millwall and John Aldridge was transferred to Oxford. We had some good years there though.

5

A ROUTINE LIFE

A LOT of what football is about is pure routine. People will say it's a great life, and they're right, it *is* a great life, you can't argue with that. But it's not necessarily an easy life. I was lucky at Plymouth because I didn't receive a lot of stick or what have you. Some players did, and a few of them couldn't handle it.

My routine? For the last few years it's been like this. On an ordinary day, I get up with the kids, take Keeley to school at 8 am, get back home, sit down, read the papers, have a cup of tea and leave for the ground. I get in for 9.45 am and have another cup of tea as training doesn't start immediately, sometimes not until 10.30 am. I'll have a little bit of a banter with the other lads, the normal sort of chit-chat, before we get down to business.

After I've taken the kids to school, I'm waiting to go to the ground; when I get to the ground and have got changed I'm waiting for training to begin, for everyone to come in. There's a lot of waiting, doing nothing in particular, in football.

To pass the time, you do silly things. Some of the lads at Argyle used to have mock fights. I'm talking about fully-grown men fighting. You get used to seeing the same people every day, just like working at the office or in a factory. But in an office or factory, you've got your job to do and everybody else has got their own job to get on with. Footballers can't do that. We have to work together with the same people for 2 or 3 hours, so nothing starts until everyone's there.

What do you talk about from one day to the next? There's a lot of macho bullshit about women, for a start, and you might talk about golf, which is very popular among footballers. But most of the talk is about football, either at your own club or somewhere else, especially when there's a lot going on.

I've seen a lot of people come into football and find it too hard to cope with mentally and physically, find it too difficult to condition their bodies to training every day of the week. I've been doing it 18 years and the older you get, the harder it is. People think it's easy but it's not. Take the example of John Aldridge, for instance. It took him 12 months to get used to it. He'd been working while he was playing part-time with South Liverpool, and all he was used to was training twice a week in the evenings. Ask John Brimacombe about it. He found it hard going for the first six months because being full-time with Plymouth Argyle was a totally different experience from working in a dockyard and playing non-league football part-time.

When you train full-time you are talking about a daily two hours of physical work which you put everything into. I wear sweatbags and every piece of kit available, just to get a good sweat on. I have to have that. I lose seven or eight pounds of weight in a training session, and it really does drain me if it's a hard session. But because I am used to it and have been doing it some time, it's easier for me than for some others. Not easy, but easier than for anyone coming in to it fresh.

Coaches will tell you that it's easy when you're a kid because you can run all day, but it becomes progressively harder as you get older. It should get easier, but it doesn't because you've got to work harder to reach your fitness level. The only way you get fit is by running. If there was any easier way, you'd do it.

I've been at six clubs and there's only three or four things I've learnt at all those clubs which I'll use myself in training. Bobby Smith, who is now coach at Cardiff City, introduced a routine when he was coach at Newport which was very hard work, but good because it didn't involve just running. It was a circuit which he invented himself that involved little shuttles, sit-ups and, the worse thing of the lot, lifting a crossbar in pairs. It was only about ten exercises, but it was very demanding. You were really tired by the end if you put everything into it

As I mentioned before, there's a saying in football which I didn't understand when I was young lad. It's simply that you get out of the game as much as you put into it. I never realised what that meant for too long. But I do now. And it's dead right. If you work hard and put everything into the game - and I'm talking about working hard, not just keeping fit - you get something out in the end. You get it from your success and the other things that come because of success.

Liverpool's training routine is legendary. They are still doing the same training they were doing when I left there in 1977. Thirteen years later and they're still doing fundamentally the same thing, very basic training. At Lincoln, every Monday and Tuesday it was just running. You'd never see a ball there. It was totally different at Liverpool. You'd do a certain amount of running - short, sharp stuff - and plenty of ball-work, with a five-a-side at the end. Ask yourself, who's the most successful club?

I went through a stage at Lincoln, after I left Sheffield Wednesday, when I did not enjoy going into training. I normally love training but I didn't enjoy it because it was all physical work. There was no enjoyment in it. As far as I am concerned, you are a football *player*. You play with a ball. Alright, you've got to keep your fitness up, and there's nothing wrong in training for that, but for five days-a-week at Lincoln it seemed like it was simply running and on a Friday morning you just might see a football. Then they'd expect you to go out on Saturday and play good football.

You can overtrain. I never realised that until I went there, but you can. You just burn out. Instead of being at peak fitness you go over the top and become tired and feel like you do when you are unfit. You do too much. The process can happen quite quickly. The easiest thing in the world is to lose your fitness and when you do, it's hard to get it back.

The soccer factory

With certain managers, you know what you're going to do week-in, week-out, and on Wednesday morning with Len Ashurst at Newport you knew you were going to have a practice match. Liverpool do it if they haven't got a midweek match. Reserves against the first-team, and the reserves always win.

With Ken Brown at Plymouth, if he was putting cones out, you knew you were going to be in a circle doing some kind of function. It might have been heading, it might have been passing but you knew it was going to be some kind of special function.

In contrast, David Kemp's training methods are geared to setting patterns of play. He works a lot on set pieces, free-kicks and corners, and they have begun to be successful. Last season, we might have practised four different corners and ten or a dozen free-kicks, and if a new fellow arrived, he was expected to have learnt them in time for his first game.

There's no variation with David Kemp's style. It's never off-the-cuff, always dictated by the rule-book. Black and white with no options. It's a percentage game and he believes in it. He and his new coach, Alan Gillett are not only bringing new ideas to the club, they are bringing new ideas to each other. At certain times, they are not exactly of one mind.

He's not a bawler and a shouter in training. You never get a rollicking, it's never nasty. He's lost his rag during some matches, mind you.

I like to know what I'm going to do in training and so do a lot of players. They don't like to train for two hours without knowing what's going to happen next. For years, the first thing we did at Plymouth every morning was ask the coach, Martin Harvey what we were going to do and the first thing he replied was: "Run the legs off you" which he said every day.

You know you're going to do warm-ups and that becomes so boring it's untrue. You know that for 40-odd weeks of the year you are going to do the same warm-up every morning, five or six mornings a week, and it becomes mundane. It's like a factory. We have a saying, if we've had a boring, quiet, day in training - "Another day over in the soccer factory." Overall, it's a great life and I love it, but it gets you that way sometimes.

It's sometimes hard to get yourself up for training during the week and it's equally difficult for the coaches to gee you up. It just becomes boring at times. I'm talking about doing exactly the same things every day, five days-a-week, with the same people, the same 20 or 30 professionals.

Len Ashurst would occasionally organise a five-a-side competition with physical contact and everything. Ken Brown wouldn't do that at Plymouth. It was very rare that he allowed tackling. Confrontations between team-mates can happen when you allow physical contact because you get hurt if you don't go in hard for a tackle. So you've got to go in hard, even if they're your own team-mates.

Saturdays are great. Players like Saturdays, or Wednesdays if you've got a game, because a match is different from the routine of training. They're what your life is all about. On a Saturday, I get up, watch a bit of telly, go to the ground, get psyched up for the match and do the business. Whether you have a good, bad or indifferent game, you have a few drinks afterwards and maybe go out that night.

After training I come back to the house and if I haven't got anything specific to do I just sit around. If it's peeing down with rain, you can't play golf or go out. What can you do? Play snooker, mooch around town, perhaps? It's not very inspiring. I think players ought to be allowed to do another job two or three afternoons a week, as long as it's not a physical job where you run the risk of injury. Maybe an office job or a driving job, something to change the routine. I know it sounds daft, but all I do after training is come home and sit and watch rubbish television, especially when it's raining.

It's very hard to come in and watch telly or videos every day. It's a perk of the job to have so much relaxation time, I suppose, but after about a month you get totally fed up. The trouble is that you get so used to it that if I have to give up the game and work for a living it will hit me so hard. John Brimacombe says he couldn't go back and work in the dockyard now.

I know a lot of players who want to work or go on courses during the football season but can't because the club won't allow it. I'm sure that you could work in addition to playing, especially in the winter months when you haven't got much to do, whether it's coaching kids or working for someone else. I would enjoy it and I know a lot of other players would too.

The worst thing about doing nothing for eight to ten hours every afternoon and evening is that you can't sleep when you go to bed. Also, having so much free time can put a hell of a strain on marriages, especially if the couple hasn't got kids and the wife doesn't work. Ten hours every day is a long time to be together, probably too long.

It boils down to boredom in the end; you've got nothing to do. What is there that a footballer can do for a hobby? You can't go motor racing or scrambling, because it's too dangerous. You can play squash, if you like it, or you can have a game of snooker or pool, but that boils down to going into licensed premises and temptation to whittle away the time drinking.

Taking the edge off

Everything is geared to Saturday, or Tuesday or Wednesday night, but every match is not the same. Sometimes you go in and the lads are all taking the micky out of each other and it's a really happy-go-lucky atmosphere. Then 2.45 pm comes around and suddenly it becomes deadly serious. Other times you go in and everyone is a little bit pensive right away.

Different people react to games in different ways. Roy Evans, who's now coach at Liverpool, was violently sick before every game when I played with him at Liverpool reserves. He used to make himself ill because he was so nervous.

Some mornings before a match I should stay locked in a room on my own, because I have a go at the kids for running around and sometimes I have a go at my missus because I'm so keyed up, especially if it's an important game. I'm not normally the nervous type - I think the most nervous I've ever been is when Newport played Carl Zeiss Jena in the European Cup-Winners Cup - but it gets to me. When you get to the ground, and there are queues of people waiting for autographs, a little bit of the edginess disappears.

Everyone has a different way of getting ready for the match. I used to wait until 2.30 pm but when I was Argyle captain I was ready by 2.15 pm because then you have to go to the referee's room to take the team sheets down and get instructions from the man in black. I know players who, as soon as they come in, whether it's 1.45 pm or 2 pm, start to get ready and are sitting around in their kit for an hour before kick-off. Other players just sit around, having a cup of tea or whatever.

My routine of a Saturday morning is to always have a breakfast after I've got up because I don't have a pre-match meal; watch a bit of telly; iron my own shirts, because I don't like my missus ironing them; have a bath, shave, and sit around in my dressing gown for the rest of the morning.

When I get to the ground at about 1.30 pm, I sort out some tickets for friends and get to the dressing room. Then I'll have a cup of tea and get changed, do my bits and bobs, tape up my rings. Martin Harvey used to have to give me a rub down every game when we were at Argyle together, so that came next for a number of seasons. Then sometimes I'll go out, do a warm-up, check my studs - an apprentice should always check with me on Friday what studs I want and whether I need new laces - and wait until 3 pm.

Like a never-ending party

The first thing a normal person does after getting paid - and sorting out the bills - is to go out. But footballers can't. We have to wait until Saturday night because we're not supposed to go out 48 hours before a match. During the summer break, the one night I enjoy going out is Friday simply because I can't go out on a Friday during the season, and it's a good night to go out.

Christmas is a total bore because you have to be careful to watch what you eat and drink. You can't tuck into the traditional five pounds of spuds, leg of turkey and Christmas pud. I just have a reasonable-sized dinner, a glass of wine to go with it, and a can of lager, and that's it. And you know that everyone else is having a few drinks, enjoying themselves. Christmas Eve is normally two nights before a match, so you can't go out and celebrate that either.

The family still enjoys Christmas. The older you get, the more you realise that Christmas is for the kids, nothing more or nothing less, and I'm lucky I've still got kids who enjoy the magic of Christmas. I get my enjoyment just from watching them open their presents. Training on Christmas Day is normal. I haven't had a Christmas Day off for ten years.

Everyone else has Bank Holidays off but professional footballers don't. We're in training, or even playing. Everyone has Easter Holidays off, but we're training then too. Alright, we have ten weeks off in the summer and people reckon you just let yourself go, but you can't or else you'll just get fat. Life's harder in the summer, if you don't train, than it is during the season. You can eat and drink what you want during the season because you are training every day and burning it off. In the summer, you don't.

I hate pre-season. I hate friendlies, especially against non-league sides when you're on a hiding to nothing. In the summer, I'll have a month off completely and that'll do me because I get totally bored otherwise. I start running again, but running on your own is never enough. You still find it hard when you go back to work because then you're competing against other people. It's hard for me at the moment to keep a certain level of fitness because of my age.

It's a good life but it's not what everyone makes out, especially at the lower levels. The lower down you go, the worse it is. It's not all glory, unless you're successful. At Plymouth, we tasted a little bit of success when we reached the FA Cup semi-final. That was brilliant, like a never-ending party. The bread-and-butter everyday games are like the day after a party. If you're not doing well, people don't want to know you.

I've know players who are very, very superstitious. Tony Toms, when he was the Sheffield Wednesday trainer, was the scruffiest person I've ever seen in my life. Once he came in with an odd pair of socks on, one brown and one black, and because we were on an unbeaten eight-match run, he never changed those socks. I mean, he washed them but he wouldn't stop wearing them until we lost. I don't like to change my boots if I'm having a good season and scoring goals, which sometimes means I'm wearing an old pair because you normally get through two match pairs a season.

I can't remember whether it was Chris Harrison or Gordon Staniforth who wore the same suit before every round of Plymouth's 1983/84 FA Cup run, but it shows how superstitious people can be. Jimmy Case, at Liverpool, always put his left boot on before his right one and there are hundreds of players who indulge in their own personal little lucky routine every weekend.

At Plymouth, the pre-match routine was very similar for all the players. They all got changed together, more or less at the same time. But Rhys Wilmot doesn't do a warm-up - sometimes I did, sometimes I didn't - and people like Mark Stuart and Kenny Brown would go out and mess about with the ball, just for something to do, rather than sit around. Jokers? We had about 12 of them in the side. Adrian Burrows was the quietest fellow I'd ever met in my life when he first came down to Plymouth and now he's another joker in the pack like the rest. He takes the mick out of everyone. He's got a very dry sense of humour and if he's in the mood he'll take the mick the whole time. Rhys is a great micky-taker, too.

Shades, Adrian Burrows, is also the worst dresser in the world. You get a lot pranks played because of what people wear. If someone comes in wearing a new pair of shoes, someone else will wait until he's gone out and then hang them from the ceiling in the middle of the dressing room for everyone to see.

Russell Coughlin started giving everyone outrageous nicknames at Argyle. Leigh Cooper has got really hairy armpits so Russ started calling him the Gibbon and that's stuck with him. While we were away on tour in Cornwall once, Adrian Burrows and John Brimacombe bought a blow-up gorilla and a blow-up skeleton, which was meant to represent Kevin Summerfield, and walked round town with them pretending they were Coops and Summers. But underneath all the joking, you have the resentment. It's there and people know about it.

Certain people do certain things together, play golf or whatever. At Plymouth, we didn't have a really big age range. There was maybe about five or six players around the age of 30 and the rest were in their 20s. We didn't have many youngsters in their teens. We were all quite adult, so there was no real problem getting on because we were all at the same level. You get some dressing rooms where the youngsters stay together and the older players stay together, and never the twain shall meet.

Indifferent welcomes

It's bound to create a bit of a stir when the manager buys new players. Imagine you're the club's right-winger and the manager spends £150,000 on a new right-winger. Your first reaction is: "What's going to happen to me?" You know he's got to justify spending the £150,000, so the chances are you'll be on your bike. Your next move is to go and see the gaffer and ask him what's going on. I've been lucky. Most clubs I've been at haven't bought anyone who looks like he's been bought to replace me, so I don't really know from personal experience what that situation's like.

The general reaction when new players come in is indifference really, because you don't know what's going to happen next or what the player is like. At Plymouth, we always tried to make new players welcome and people seemed to settle in very well. The players at Plymouth when I first arrived didn't make me welcome at all. The club used to own a cottage near the ground which I stayed in after I signed and sometimes I sat in my room alone, every night of the week. I used to eat on my own and go out on my own. In the end I bought a telly and sat in watching that.

There were maybe one or two players - one was Gordon Staniforth - who said: "Come round to my place and have a beer" or something. That was part of the reason that I wanted to leave the club - because I couldn't believe that the players did not go out together socially. They might have a drink after the match, but that was all, and I resented that. Now, if any new player arrives at the club, people make a point of saying: "Come round to my house." The worst thing in the world is being on your own, sitting in your digs or hotel or whatever, not knowing anyone. I resented the fact that no-one invited me round to their house or asked me out for a beer when I first came to Plymouth. I literally sat in the club cottage five nights a week.

I was in digs with a couple following my move to Sheffield Wednesday from Liverpool and after that I bought my own place, so there wasn't a problem because it was my choice. I stayed living in Sheffield when I moved to Lincoln, which wasn't the right thing to do, and at Newport I shared a place with a guy called Neil Bailey until we sold our house in Sheffield and Elaine moved down.

But when I first came to Plymouth, I rented four different houses in the initial two years I was here and that was another mistake. I should have bought my own place right away but I couldn't sell the house in Newport at first, and should have bought a place in Plymouth when I eventually did. Probably, I might not have moved on if I had.

When footballers come down to the Westcountry, they generally feel isolated because of its location. It's not as if you can hop in the car and drive for a couple of hours to see your parents. If you come from London or the North, it's maybe four or five hours away and you don't like making those sort of trips regularly. It's very hard, especially for wives or girlfriends.

If you're a player you've got a few friends at the club you're okay, you can go out for beer or whatever, but your wife's left sitting in the house on her own and it's lonely for her. Even lonelier if she doesn't work or hasn't got kids to occupy her time.

Two wasted days

Travelling is boring, especially on some of the away trips when you've got a six-hour coach trip and you're sitting in a traffic-jam for two hours because the times you travel you always hit the motorway trouble-spots at their busiest times. If Plymouth went to Leeds, say, we always managed to hit Birmingham, which isn't the easiest place to negotiate, at lunchtime, meaning we were virtually stationary for two hours.

Then when you get to the hotel and sit down for a supposedly nice meal, you find it's absolute crap. You feel absolutely horrible because you've been sitting on the coach all this time and you seem to have been eating and drinking from the moment you get on until the moment you get off. It's boredom. You get a packed lunch, three or four sandwiches, an apple or orange, and a Kit-Kat or Mars bar, and you've got coffee and soft drinks on the coach. Because there's little else to do, you end up eating all this gunge, whereas if you were at home you might have a sandwich and coffee and a biscuit and that would be it. Boredom does strange things to you.

Some of the lads will arrive at the hotel with square eyes because they've been watching videos all the way up. They'll watch them all the way back as well. Even playing cards all the way up becomes a little bit monotonous and routine, but there's nothing else to do.

To a lot of people, the idea of staying the night in an expensive hotel might sound glamorous but honestly only one in three is worth it. Some meals are absolute rubbish. You've got 14 lads and we've been at places where we've sat down to eat at 7 pm and haven't been served for three-quarters of an hour. And when the meals arrive they are not worth waiting for.

When I'm at home on a Friday night I'll usually have steak, mush-rooms and chips. Standard footballers' fare. In a hotel the menu is full of meals with all these rich sauces, which is the last thing you want the night before a game. So you ask for something simple that isn't on the menu, like steak, fish, or chicken and they refuse unless you are on the a la carte menu, which is £20 instead of £12.95. Carveries are alright, though.

Staying in hotels is not as glamorous as it might seem. There is simply nothing to unless they've got a leisure centre where you can go for a swim or or a sauna. You can't do anything too physical because there's a game next day and if the hotel's got a snooker or pool table, it's normally in the bar, which is forbidden territory.

You arrive between 5.30 pm and 7.00 pm, have a cup of tea and a shower and wait until mealtime. It's different at home where you'll either help the missus making the tea, or keep the kids from under her feet while she does it.

After the meal you go back to your room, maybe phone the wife and then you're set for three hours of total boredom. Guess what we do? Play cards, about five or six of us, normally in my room, until 11 pm when it's time to bed down.

Different people have different routines. Kenny Brown would get his head down at 11 pm and sleep through until noon the next day. No-one would see him until it was time to check out. When I was rooming with John Matthews, we never missed a breakfast. Never had a pre-match meal though. Some will get up at 9 am and have breakfast, go for a walk, have a shower, watch telly and come down for pre-match tea and toast or whatever's prescribed.

I rarely do that. I have a full breakfast and go for a walk around the hotel grounds and come back to read the papers. The glamour, if you can call it that, is because it's all laid on a plate for you, you don't have to do anything. Your bed's made up for you, your meals are cooked, and they are decent hotels. But underneath that you've got two days of monotony, doing nothing.

Since David Kemp has taken over at Plymouth, the pre-match meal has always been chicken and pasta, the steak and chips and what-have-you have all gone. Chicken and pasta now, which I believe is supposed to give you energy.

He's also introduced a new warm-up routine for away matches which consists of about ten minutes running and stretching on the pitch an hour or so before the kick-off. It's okay for the younger players but my legs stiffened up when I sat down afterwards and I had to get in the bath to get them loose again. I think it's a waste of time because it's too early. But he's the manager and he knows exactly what he wants. If anyone doesn't want to fit into his plans then he will bring in players that do.

After the match, we have a couple of drinks and then get the fish and chips in. We can stop off if we want but we normally opt for the fish and chips because it means we can get home quicker. If we're on the coach by 5.30 pm and you know you've got five hours worth of journey in front of you, you don't really want to make the weekend any longer by stopping off for a meal.

Apart from the actual football, it's two wasted days. Nearly 48 hours of doing nothing to play 90 minutes of football, that is what it's all about. Apart from about three trips, Plymouth travel to away matches the day before, so that's at least 20 matches a season that they're on the road for. West Bromwich Albion stay away about three times a season because they are pretty local for everywhere.

But you've got to stay away if you're travelling for more than three-and-a-half or four hours. Sometimes we'd leave Plymouth at noon and not arrive at the hotel until eight in the evening. Eight hours in a coach! I would think at times that sort of itinerary must affect your performance. It's hard to continually travel and not feel any effects.

I also think that's why a lot of players think twice before coming to Plymouth to play. Doing nothing is surprisingly very tiring. Ask anyone who does a lot of travelling and they'll tell you the same thing. I don't know why it is but that's the way. And the likes of Plymouth, Torquay and Exeter are on the road every other week and sometimes twice in a week.

For a midweek evening game, the routine is to have lunch in a hotel and go to sleep around 2 pm for a couple of hours. It's never a deep sleep, it's a different kind, a sort of dozy sleep. You might wake up three or four times. Some players can't sleep at all. I'm not a great afternoon sleeper so sometimes the night before I go to bed late to try and help me go to sleep the following afternoon.

You don't sleep properly but you've got to have the rest. You always feel refreshed after you've had a rest and a shower and you put some clean gear on. I always feel great afterwards. Smart, relaxed and ready for a a hard game of football.

Colin Addison at Newport used to say that your rest is as good as your training and he is absolutely right. You can't go wallpapering or cutting the bushes on a Friday afternoon because you've got to have your reserves of energy for the following day.

When you sleep in the afternoon before an evening game you are building up for what is to come. You always get tired in a game. Games are totally different from training. You should put more effort into a game than you do your training because the game is your be all and end all. Those 90 minutes are what you are geared up for.

Happiness is....: Celebrating a goal with David Byrne.

Kept out: Thwarted by Swindon Town goalkeeper Fraser Digby at Home Park.

In at the deep end: Endurance training with the Royal Marines.

Eyes down: Shielding the ball from an opponent.

Referee...: Sometimes decisions never go your way.

Outnumbered: Taking on the Stoke City defence single-handed.

Best foot foward: On the move against Barnsley.

The thrill of it all: Enjoying a goal with Kevin Hodges and the Plymouth fans.

6

ON A PEDESTAL

YOU'D GO berserk if you listened to some of the things people tell you. I've had letters from people telling me to pack the game in. I know I've been lucky in Plymouth and I had a good, and loyal, personal following, but you can never please all of thc people all of the time. Everyone's got their knockers. I have, everyone has.

Some of the stories you hear are unbelievable. When I was in Sheffield and going out with Elaine, she became pregnant. We'd both got our divorces through and were going to get married. So I was out with Elaine, and her cousin, who resembled Elaine and also happened to be pregnant, was with us. We went to a place called the Stonehouse, me with a pregnant woman on each arm, and it caused a bit of a stir. The next thing I knew was that there was a story doing the rounds in Sheffield along the lines that I'd got both of them pregnant. Honestly. That's the sort of thing that happens.

I wonder sometimes, whether, when I was in Sheffield, some of the girls I went out with just went out with me because I was a nice fellow, or because I was good looking, or because I was Tommy Tynan.

Sheffield is a big place with two teams that generate at least 25,000 fans each. It's a working-class place and the people there love their football, so if you were a a footballer with Sheffield Wednesday or Sheffield United, you were well-known and it was easy for players to get a reputation if they went out. I went out and I had a reputation, which, from the outside looking in, was probably justified.

But for every six stories told about me, only a conservative two were ever true. In Sheffield, there's a night-club called Josephine's and it's a bit of a high-class night-club. If you can't pull in there you can't pull anywhere. I used to go there on the two best nights of the week, Wednesday, which was the last night we were allowed to drink before match day, and Saturday, after the game.

Before I met Elaine, I'd go out to this club and after a few drinks, I'd inevitably come out with a different bird every night. That went on for about eight or nine months but although the birds stopped when I went out with Elaine on a regular basis, the stories didn't. I don't know how many women I've been to bed with but if I went with twenty I bet you ten of them only went with me because I was Tommy Tynan, probably even more.

A couple of years ago, Steve Cooper and I came out of Home Park after training. There were two girls waiting outside and one of them said to us: "Is Tommy Tynan still in there?" So Coops told her that I was Tommy Tynan and she didn't believe him. She said: "Not that's not him. That's not the fellow I met." It turned out she'd met this fellow in Bristol the previous Saturday night who told her that he was me and she'd gone out with him, and probably more.

Restrictive practices

Some of the stories that do the rounds about me are true, but a lot of them aren't. If I believed everything I heard about myself I'd go scatty. To most people, a footballer leads a glamorous life, and to a certain extent it is glamorous - I'd never change what I've done - but there's a lot of monotony and boredom and a lot of things you have to give up, things that normal people do, but you can't do.

You cannot do certain things, and that can become very restrictive.

There was a time in a Plymouth restaurant that my wife had to stop me having a go at the owner. We were in this restaurant, with friends, and were told we'd have to wait half-an-hour for a table. I said that was alright, bought some drinks, and picked up a plate of mints from the bar and put them on the table we were sitting at.

The owner said: "You can't put those there." So I told him I thought he was being petty, picked up a handful of mints and put the plate back on the bar. Then he told us he wouldn't serve us and I got up to have a go at him. My missus shouted: "Don't" and pulled me away. If I'd had a go and someone found out, that would have been in the papers.

I was banned from driving in 1989 for speeding. Some people high up in the Plymouth police have told me that I was stopped because of who I am. It's easy to tell becacuse of the sponsored plates.

Alright, I got banned for 28 days and I was handed a large fine. If it had been anyone else it wouldn't have made the local papers, but, because of who I am it was all over the press.

One regret I have got is not learning to drive a lot earlier. It never interested me at all when I was young. Even at Liverpool, all the apprentices learnt to drive once they were 17 but all the talk about cars just didn't stimulate me at all. If I'd passed my test a lot earlier it might have made my life easier because when I was at Sheffield I used to live in Derbyshire which meant either getting a taxi or two buses to get to the ground. Looking back at it, I can't understand how I didn't have a car. I couldn't get by without one now. When I was banned for speeding it was like having an arm cut off.

You have got to watch what you do. You very rarely go out with strangers. You go out with friends or some of the lads so that anything that happens remains between yourselves. Sometimes, there have been occasions when I've wanted to have a go at someone but had to bite my tongue. It might be alright for an ordinary person to have an argument in public, but not me. If you do and it gets a bit out of hand and the person who you are arguing with realises who you are, that could spell trouble. Some people might get a kick out of telling their mates how they'd stuck one on Tommy Tynan.

Life in a goldfish bowl

Things only very rarely annoy me. One time was when, through a third party, I'd agreed to go and sign some autographs at a school canteen in Tavistock. I totally forgot about it, and it turned out there were 200 kids there, along with the local radio station and the local press, waiting for me to turn up. Apparently, I'd been supposed to be opening this new canteen, although I'd never been told that. I thought it was just an autograph session.

The next thing that happened was that the local radio station and local paper both phoned me up, making a big thing out of it, asking me how much I'd been paid to open the canteen and why I didn't turn up. I gave one or two people a mouthful and said I'd take them to court if they ran a derogatory story.

What really annoyed me is that they weren't there the other 400-odd times I've done things in my own time. I eventually went to the school and gave them an autographed football, photos and shirt, and stayed for an hour signing autographs, but the press wasn't there then either. It was my fault, I admit that, but where were they then?

I went out for a meal at the Grecian Taverna restaurant in Plymouth one night and from the moment we walked in Elaine could hear this fellow whispering things about how I'd been banned from driving and lost my sponsored car (which I hadn't). That annoys me. I don't mind people coming up to me and saying: "Hello Tom. How you doing? Good game today" or even "Bad game today." That's fine, but when people don't do that and sit there whispering about you, you feel like you're a goldfish in a goldfish bowl. My situation is minor compared to other people more in the public eye, though.

Being a footballer is the next best thing to being a film star. People do not look at footballers, especially famous footballers, as ordinary people. They expect you to act or behave differently. I can't understand why.

I love the adulation of people and the experience of them recognising you. It's nice to be known and in many ways I'm glad I'm not just one of the faceless masses. I like the fact that when I walk around town people that I don't even know say hello to me, or being treated to a cup of coffee when I'm in a shop waiting for my wife as she's trying on clothes. It's part of being famous. When I pack it in, I'll miss it desperately and other people have told me the same thing. But that will pass and I will have to get on with my life.

Being famous gets you into places and gets you things you normally couldn't get. I'm talking about getting discounts from clothes shops, getting into night-clubs, sponsored cars, that sort of thing. I've been in a shop trying on a suit and this fellow's asked if I'd do something to help promote the shop. When I said I would, he just said: "Have the suit." I've got discounts from most of the menswear shops in Plymouth because they're happy to have Plymouth Argyle players buying their gear from their shops.

Even now, people want to know you because of who you are and what you do. Not because you're yourself but because you're a footballer playing for Plymouth Argyle or Torquay United or whoever. I don't like hangers-on, of which there are plenty in the football world, but some people like to be associated with famous people and I can understand that.

I get people who I've never known saying hello and wanting to stay in my company, talking for hours and hours. Sometimes they are quite nice and you end up buying them a drink, but others are totally boring and you have to be a bit blunt. You have to walk away. It's obvious what you are doing because you've been talking to these people for ten minutes and then you say: "Excuse me a minute, I've just got to go and see my wife" and you never come back. You know you've done it - you've got to do it - and they know that you've done it, but these people will still say hello to you next time and buy you a drink. You've been rude to them in the nicest way you can.

Post-match trauma

Plymouth is one of the few clubs that doesn't have a players' bar so after a match we'd have to go down to the Far Post, which is really a members' club. I wonder, though, how many people pay their membership subscriptions just because they know that they're going to be able to have a drink with the players afterwards?

Gordon and Shirley, who run the Far Post, are brilliant people, different class, but there are some people on the members' committee who try and lay the law down to the players about who they can bring in as guests and how many. It's been going on for years and it annoys the players. Before the FA Cup game with Everton in 1989, we were told we would only be allowed to bring in one or two people each, because it was going to be packed. As it turned out, it was half-empty.

I know one of the problems has been the kids, but players have to rely on the Far Post because Plymouth hasn't got a players' lounge. Most of the fans pay their membership because they enjoy drinking and socialising with the players. One membership subscription a year and some people think they own you, though. It's unbelievable. Football is about the fans, but sometimes they expect a little too much.

There are some people in Plymouth for who Plymouth Argyle is the whole of their lives, apart from working. Most of their money is spent on Argyle, and they live, breathe and sleep the club. It's hard to believe, I know, but there are such people. These people who go to every game, home and away, deserve it for you to give something back to them. It's great when you travel away and you see the same faces. It makes you feel like you've got a purpose. We have always given them tickets and tried to look after them as best we can.

The other way of giving something back is to socialise with them at the Far Post, but when some of these people cause hassle because you bring your wife and kids, family and friends in, it becomes a little bit fraught. It's stupid really. If it wasn't for a chap called Pete Sutton, who always tries, and manages, to sort things out, I don't know what would happen sometimes. When I was captain at Argyle, I actually spoke to Gordon on three separate occasions about players boycotting the bar, not because of him and Shirley but because we felt like second-class citizens when we were told we couldn't do this or couldn't do that. It wasn't on.

A player's wife was once stopped from going in there, and I never knew why. We never knew who had said certain people couldn't come in. It was always "the committee."

The other thing that annoys me is that I should think it's the players and their friends who spend most of the money. Most of the members are looking for somewhere to have a quick couple of pints and let the crowd drift away, but we tended to stop there for a few beers, so we were spending money. I know it's a small minority, but all you want to do is to sit there and have a few beers and talk to a few people, especially if you've had a hard game, not walk into the middle of controversy.

The club, any club, is about the fans and the players. The players should look after the fans and the fans should look after the players. If their lives are relaxed as possible, it's sure to benefit them on a Saturday afternoon.

We were all fit, all decent players, we wouldn't be there otherwise. You don't know what's going through people's minds when they are playing, though. Maybe it's not on the game. Everyone has bad games.

Joe who?

I've been fortunate with fans at most places where I've been. I've always had a good rapport with them. They've liked me mainly because I've produced the goods on the field.

There's always someone who wants to have a word with me when I go out and, because they've stood on the terraces, if I can't give them five minutes of my time then I'm acting like a bit of a prima donna. It might sound hard, but sometimes they are boring people; nevertheless, it's important to respond to them. Sometimes you're out, sitting down having a quiet drink with your wife or friends, and about five or six lads will walk in, drunk to the eyeballs, and want to talk about football. That's a bit hard. I've been with players when this sort of thing has happened and they've just told them to eff off. There was also a player at Newport who wouldn't give kids the time of day if they asked for his autograph.

Years ago, ninety-five people out of a hundred wanted to be a footballer, although nowadays it's probably down to about seven out of ten. A lot of people in showbusiness are wrapped up in football. A lot of rock stars say they would have liked to be a professional footballer if they could have.

I believe it's the next best thing to being a film or television star. Every town has a football club and you are a star in that town if you are a player with that club. You feel special, and proud when people come up to you when you're out. They don't know Joe Public, but they know Tommy Tynan.

I don't mind giving up my time to speak to people, and to sign autographs, although some supporters think that they own you because you play for their team and they pay your wages. Sometimes they think you should have time for them and them alone. You can give them a little of your time but not all of your time and for some people that's not enough. But it's hard lines because no-one can make too many demands on players' time.

You are letting them down when you're not winning. More than that, you are letting down their families because women, for instance, feel bad when their husband, or brother, or son, has seen you lose. I was shopping in Asda in Plymouth once when two old ladies, one about 50 the other about 60, came up to me. One of them said: "Saw you got beaten last night, Tom. Unlucky." She'd probably never been to a football match in her life but us losing had affected her.

I can understand the disappointment of fans. Some of them devote a lot of time to following the club. They miss meals, take time off work and spend a lot of their hard-earned money travelling round the country. For some of them, it is literally their life and although you play for the fans' pleasure you sometimes forget how much it means to some people.

Noises off

On the pitch, you hear the crowd when you first go out and all the way to the kick-off. If you get involved early on you very rarely hear the crowd after that.

There have been games when I haven't had a touch for 15 minutes and I can hear the crowd getting at me for not getting involved. Then, all of a sudden, I get a few touches and the game is what it's all about, I generally don't hear the crowd at all.

You can always hear the odd shout if there's 8,000 or 9,000 but most of the time you aren't really listening. You only hear the crowd if you're having a bad time.

The hardest thing of all is to miss a good chance and to keep on going. That's where you become a good professional really. If you get five chances in a match and you score one, everyone forgets the four you missed. It's all down to experience, but I still feel like digging a hole in the ground and getting into it if I miss a chance.

I'm a great believer in people who pay their money every week, whether it's to watch football or to have a good grouse, doing what they want because they have paid for the privilege. Whether they like what they see is entirely down to them.

A lot of people like me but I know there are a lot of people who don't rate me at all. I've got a fellow who writes to me every month and never says a bad word against me. I've had bad games, I know, but he never thinks so because he's a fan.

Everyone has their favourite. I have letters from people saying I should pack it all in. Even from Plymouth fans when I was at Home Park. You can't please all the people all the time.

It is the fans that make you a star. They have the power to make players or break them. They put you on a pedestal, and they can knock you off it as well. They have a love affair with goalscorers, that's the way football has always been. People that score goals are idols.

I'm coming to the end of my playing career and I've had a great time. People have said a lot of nice things about me, and I appreciate them. Without the fans, I wouldn't have got anything out of football. They pay my wages, not the board of directors. If they didn't pay to come through the turnstiles to watch you, the directors would have to pay you out of their own pockets and I'm sure we wouldn't be getting the wages that we're getting now if that was the case. It's all down to the fans.

I'm professional enough to know that I'm doing a job for the club and the club is, ultimately, the fans. They bring in the revenue.

I've done more than a few presentations and personal appearances because I believe that you've got to give a little of what you get from the supporters back to them.

Giving something back

When you walk round town and people recognise you, you don't mind saying hello, though it's annoying when people shout after you.

When you're out on a Saturday night having a meal with your wife and friends, you tend to get people coming up and asking for your autograph. I don't mind one or two but I can remember one time when there were about 15 people round us as we were eating, all wanting me to sign.

Then there are the times when you get people in pubs giving you stick. You can either walk away or have a go back and, nine times out of ten, having a go back is the worst thing you can do because the other fellow's normally the worse for drink. Thankfully, that's very rarely happened to me.

My daughter Tammy's had more stick than me. She goes out for a drink and gets a lot of stick just because she's Tommy Tynan's daughter. She's had a lot of hassle because of me and that's simply not fair. She's got her own life to lead.

Even Jordanna gets a little bit of it from lads at school. When Plymouth got knocked out of the FA Cup by Everton she was told: "Your dad's rubbish." But it's nothing really. You are always going to get these people.

I would rather have someone say to my face: "You played rubbish today" rather than say: "Well played, Tommy" and then go away and say to someone else you had a rubbish game. There are people like that, but I prefer to know where I stand.

It's very nice being a celebrity. I love it. I like to think I've become popular not just because of football but because of what I've done outside the game as well.

As I've said, the people pay my wages so it's nothing for me to drive to a function for half-an-hour to give them a lot of enjoyment.

I went to see a kid at a Wimpy bar, I think it was his eighth birthday, presented him with a football, did one or two photographs. I was there for only about twenty minutes and didn't take anything for it.

The next day a big bunch of flowers arrived for my wife and a bottle of Scotch for me with a note thanking me for making the lad's day. It was totally unexpected.

At the other end of the scale you get people who expect you to do things for no thanks. There's not many of them about thankfully.

I do a lot of charity work. I remember one summer there must have been flowers in my house for about six weeks. People ask you what you want and I just ask them to get my wife a bunch of flowers because she loves them.

Once I did a presentation at a non-league club called Marine. They got my wife some flowers and a tankard for me, as well as buying us drinks. There were only about a dozen people at this do and we got flowers that must have cost £15 and a tankard which must have cost the same. We didn't expect these things but these people came up with it.

On the other hand, it's possible to earn a lot of money, making personal apperances. One manager who I had dealings with told me about the personal appearances he would make and say that he'd got a black box under his bed with ten grand in it which he couldn't put in the bank because the taxman would want to know about it. I asked him about his contract and he said he got that in his hand as well. Maybe they were just a couple of his wind-ups, I don't know. I never really found out.

He was talking, maybe jokingly, about this box under his bed with ten grand in it but when his players went in to his office to try and negotiate a new contract with a two grand signing-on fee he exploded. A lot of managers who have previously been players are like that.

Being so well-known still surprises me. There was a time when I was walking along the street in Looe when this copper came up to me. I started thinking all sorts of things but then he said: "Excuse me Tommy, can I have your autograph for my girlfriend?" Even when you think you are away from it all, people recognise you.

I understand why people want to be associated with you and probably I get a lot more of it than other players. My best friends in the Westcountry are people I've known for years and they are all outside of football. All my real friends over the years have come from outside football. There's no such thing as close friendships in football. There can't be because all players are managers, they all have their own opinions about every single player.

You play a game, and if you win it doesn't matter but if you lose you look for blame. You do it instinctively. You say: "He didn't play too well" or: "The back four wasn't too clever today." Everyone does it. You become very critical. You blame someone, someone else blames you. That sort of environment doesn't make for close friendships really.

7

MONEY, THAT'S THE PROBLEM

IT'S NICE to have a few bob to be able to buy and do the sort of things that most people regard as luxuries. People think that professional footballers must be loaded but that's a load of rubbish. There are players in the Second Division who are earning absolute buttons. When I was at Plymouth, I knew someone working in insurance who earnt more than I did.

When you look at it you can say it is good money for the hours that you actually put in. It is, but the team has got to win it's home games for me to keep the standard of living that I have set for myself and my family because then we collect good bonuses. If we're not winning, I am not exaggerating to say we have to scrimp and save for the little luxuries, even with Elaine working three days-a-week. And I mean that.

I was lucky when I was at Plymouth. One or two people gave me a sponsored car, which meant I could save a lot of money that could go towards something else. People look at me and say: "There goes Tommy Tynan, a professional footballer who drives a sponsored car. What a great life he's got." It *is* a great life but people do not realise that it does become boring. Everything is geared to the football, but you only play a match once, sometimes twice, a week. The rest of it is not what it's cracked up to be. If there's something I can make a few bob from then I'll do it.

At Plymouth, I got a lot of things that other players didn't get simply because I was captain. Some of the stuff I had through a sponsorship deal with the sportswear company, Hummel, was tremendous. Other players didn't get that. But I didn't sit around and wait for it to come to me. I went out and got it.

I've got to be selfish because I want a good standard of living. If you can make money from outside the game as well as by playing it, you've got it made.

You've got to look after yourself, and your wife and family, first and foremost. You don't go and see the manager to talk about someone else's contract, you go in and talk to him about your own contract. If one player is getting £500-a-week and another is getting £450-a-week, that's down to the player's demands and what he's prepared to accept. The resentment starts when you sign a contact you're happy with but six months later you find someone else is on £50-a-week more than you.

Greed in the dictionary is defined as an excessive desire for something, whether it's goals, money or whatever. Everyone tries to get as much as they can. At the level of football I've played, there have been one or two players who've asked for ridiculous money and they've always had to back down. But you can't blame them for asking for it. In every job, people always ask for more than they are eventually prepared to accept. There are a lot of greedy players in the game, but I think they are always accused of being greedy after the fact. If someone gets a large signing-on fee, other players might accuse him of being a greedy beggar but they say that because they didn't get what they asked for. That's life.

Budgeting for success

In football, you should never tell anyone what you're earning because it causes animosity when word gets back to the dressing room. If I go in and negotiate a £100-a-week rise and some signing-on money and one of my team-mates accepts less because it's more than he was hoping for -

even though it's less - and it later comes out that you're on more than him, he resents you.

I think, that to within about £50-a-week, all the players at any club should be on the same money, and maybe even £50 difference is too much. Gordon Nisbet, the Plymouth defender, used to say he didn't care if they paid someone £1,000-a-week as long as the player was better than those we already had at the club and he helped us to win promotion.

That's a very selfless attitude. But if he does help you win promotion, you are in a good position to go in and see the boss and say: "I'm one of the players who helped us earn promotion. I think I deserve more money." If I work with someone and they tell me they're on £20-a-week more than me I think: "So what?"; if they're on £100-a-week more than me, that's different.

At Plymouth, there wasn't too much resentment over money, but the club is not one of the best payers in the Second Division. When we played Bradford two years ago, their best player was on a £500 basic weekly wage and had been given a £20,000 signing-on fee to re-sign for the club. I don't think there's any way that Plymouth would have paid that money at that time.

That's the problem. Plymouth is one of the better clubs around. It's got a lovely ground and a huge potential catchment area. Ever since I came to the Westcountry, people have been saying to me that if the directors were prepared to speculate to accumulate then the club could get somewhere. But I don't think they will because the club has had it's fingers burnt in the past and is wary of the risks.

I think Plymouth is a decent club and it can be the best in the Second Division......if it really wants to be. Ken Brown was building for the future and spent wisely on players from a limited budget. All the players Ken Brown bought were happy. They all got a decent signing-on fee and were all on decent money. Which is the way it should be. David Kemp will have to maintain that situation and build on it.

But Plymouth directors and managers will have to spend money if the club wants to compete with the likes of Leeds and Newcastle. Bradford didn't have a great deal of money but they paid their players well because they knew they had one or two players that were assets. There are one or two players at Plymouth who are assets, and who could realise a lot of money in the future.

Without getting success, there's no other sure-fire way of generating money. Plymouth Argyle's first year in the First Division, when it comes, is going to generate £1 million. It's a shame you've got to sell your best player, but if that raises the money for two or three others of a decent standard it is simply good business. I think it's sad, but that's the way it is. Bringing on young players at Plymouth is difficult because the reserve league they play in, the Western League, is rubbish compared to, say, the Football Combination or the Central League. The only way of bringing on the youngsters at Plymouth is to play them in the first-team, and that is not always possible. You can put one or two in here and there but, that way, it is going to take a long time before you know whether they are good enough to make it or not.

I'm afraid money is one of the biggest problems in football. Clubs have to have a lot of it to survive and be successful, because every year their wage bill will rise as players demand more money for making the side a successful one. Probably the worst thing that happened for clubs was the players' right to freedom of contract and the abolition of the minimum wage.

Shrinking squads

Finances govern a lot of players' minds but it's a short life and you've got to make as good a living as you can in that limited time. It's not as if you can carrying on playing until you are 40 or 50. The average finishing age is probably about 32 and then that's it, no more football.

I'd still be playing football part-time if I had a job. I'd play every week, without a shadow of a doubt. Do all the travelling, everything. For love. If football was a semi-professional sport, I'd still play. Even through all the bad times I had at Lincoln and Newport, if I'd packed it in then and got a job I would have played for someone at some level.

I don't know whether I could play non-league football after I leave the professional game, though. Not because I wouldn't want to carry on playing football but because I've set myself standards and I feel that non-league level is outside those standards.

Even if the game was amateur, I'd still play football. You are a professional simply because you are the best at what you do and people are willing to pay you for doing what you're good at. It's as basic as that. There are not a lot of professional footballers, about 2,000, which is a very small percentage of the male population.

There were a lot of good players around when I was a kid but there's definitely not the wealth of talent around today that there was then. In that respect, I was lucky to make the grade. I think it would have been easier for me if I was just starting out.

Outside the First Division and a few clubs in the Second, the game is all about finances. The Third and Fourth Divisions are totally dominated by financial considerations. Keeping within a strict budget.

When I was at Sheffield Wednesday, they had a squad of 34 professionals, and they were in the Third Division. You're lucky if you get that half that sort of squad in the lower divisions these days. When I was at Rotherham, they only had 18 professionals and everyone was paid the same money, decent wages. There were also about ten fringe players on less money. Lower division clubs cannot keep big squads and they are now helped to some extent by the Youth Training Scheme, which means they can have young players for two years and all they have to pay for are their digs.

But clubs are only turning to YTS because it eases the financial burden. I hate it when kids are referred to as YTS lads. They are apprentice professional footballers. They are governed by the same rules and regulations as the professionals and they should act in exactly the same way. At the same time, they should look up to the senior professionals which, unfortunately, they don't.

Superleagues and megabucks

It would be great to have a British League but I can't see that happening. I think what will happen eventually is that there will be a Super League of English clubs, and a First Division, a Second Division and so on. People within the game are looking after themselves and their money. What they are saying is: "We're going to get all the big money and the smaller clubs will have to scrap it out and pick up what they can get."

The bigger clubs will get even bigger and the only way the smaller clubs can improve themselves will be by success, which generates money, or by getting hold of two or three players that will be worth a lot of money, selling them for a huge profit and using the extra cash to buy lesser players, but more of them, who can bring you success. Sell a couple of players for a million quid and buy five or six others to strengthen your squad and get promotion.

At the end of the day, Third and Fourth Division clubs, where I've spent a majority of my career, have a hard life, and it will get even harder when a Super League comes around. You'll see the same teams on telly every week and no-one else. It's nearly reached that stage now. ITV didn't drop into the Second Division for their goals round-up when there were no First Division games on Saturdays during last season, did they? It's as if we didn't exist.

There should be regionalised Saturday night or Sunday afternoon highlights, with people in the South West seeing all the Devon clubs, the Bristols and maybe even the Welsh clubs.

I think the transfer market has gone absolutely berserk and we should have taken a leaf out of the continentals' book and put a price-ceiling on it. Another thing the continentals do is to give a player a third of the transfer fee. I'd rather see that and a maximum wage re-introduced. I know a player gets a signing-on fee in this country but that can be a relatively small percentage of the actual transfer.

The situation has occurred when a club has been willing to pay £50,000 for me but they can't afford the wages I want. They are willing to pay the money to the club, but not to me, and we're not talking astronomical sums. An extra £50-a-week or an extra few grand signing-on fee. They weren't willing to look after me and I think that's wrong.

You're only worth what someone is willing to pay for you. If someone's willing to pay £20,000 for you, that's what you're worth; if someone's willing to pay £1 million for you, then you're worth a million. Having said that, there are some very lucky players in football who have been grossly overvalued. On the other hand, I've always proved that I can score goals yet I've never cost more than £55,000.

You can't offer £250,000 for a player and expect him to play for wages of £200-a-week. These things have to be in proportion, which is why Plymouth Argyle never spend lots of money on a player. If they could afford the fee, they could not satisfy the player's demands without upsetting their wage structure - even with a signing-on fee (which you pay tax on) or an ex gratia payment (which you don't).

I've been lucky. I've had one or two signing-on fees and ex gratia payments, but without them I wouldn't have signed. And I don't know why the taxman is suddenly getting interested in these ex gratia payments. Businessmen have been doing it for years. A pay-off when you move to another club is not necessarily a loyalty bonus or whatever the press make it out to be: it's your money, and you're entitled to it when you leave a club.

If you sign for a club and the manager says you will be getting £15,000 now plus another £10,000 spread over two years and you get transferred at the end of the first year, you've only got £20,000 of the £25,000 you were promised when you signed. If it's loyalty money, you should see out your contract. Fortunately, it's never happened to me. I've always got my money whenever I've been transferred.

Transfer fees are never as simple as the public is led to believe. If a player costs £100,000, the buying club would have to pay £100,000 plus 15 per cent Value Added Tax, plus five per cent to the league, plus a signing-on fee to the player. So the actual money paid out is nearer £140,000. Imagine what happens when the fee is £600,000. The actual money you're shelling out is around £700,000.

8

SELF-PRESERVATION

THERE HAVE been people at Plymouth who could have pushed me for my place if they had wanted to, but they seemed to be waiting for me to retire or move on. I wouldn't have hung around if it had been me in their position.

If I was left out of the side when I was a teenager I'd wait two or three weeks and then go in and see the gaffer about the future. That's self-preservation. Looking after yourself, not anyone else. If he said I didn't figure in the club's planning then it was up to me to get on my bike and make a living for my family. I think that's why I've had seven clubs. I couldn't stand being out of the side for longer than a month. I just couldn't stomach it.

It's very frustrating when you're out of the team but scoring goals for the reserves and you think you should be in the side. It's worse when you're out of the side and you know other clubs want you but you can't do anything about it because you're under contract.

Colleagues at Plymouth had a little joke at my expense about my out-of-season running routine, but that's self-preservation too. I'm keeping my fitness up. In Porthleven on a pre-season Cornish tour with Argyle, we were given a day-off. Some of the lads hung around doing nothing in particular, some went fishing and I went running. I know they thought I was mad to be running on my day off but I was looking after myself.

Football is a pressure game, whether you're at the top or at the bottom. The worst thing is to be easy-osey in the middle. Pressure has destroyed players. Fans have destroyed players.

The Plymouth crowd's reaction to winger Dougie Anderson was a standing joke among the Argyle players. We used to call it the boo-ometer. I get nerves on the odd occasion but I couldn't stand going out to play knowing that there's 5,000 fans waiting to have a go at you, like they were waiting for Dougie. Dougie would do ever so well in training and reserve games, but as soon as Saturday afternoon came and the fans started having a go, that was it, he was finished.

I'm lucky, I've never had that sort of reaction, apart from a little bit at Lincoln when I wasn't doing the business. But it is a pressure game and you've got to be able to handle the pressure.

A manager tries not to put pressure on you, but there's pressure from all sides. People don't realise that Saturday afternoon is just a small part of your life and that football is not always your main concern in life. When the fans see you playing, they don't think that maybe you're a month behind with the mortgage and that four or five bills have landed on your doormat that morning, or that your little girl's in hospital with a broken leg, or that your wife's unhappy living away from her parents. People think: "He's a footballer, all he's got to do is play football."

There's pressure from outside the game, too. There was a Plymouth player who got nothing but hassle from his wife, who didn't like the area and didn't like the club, from the moment he got home after training until the moment he left for the ground next day. In her opinion, everyone at the club was just a bunch of effing so-and-sos. She wanted to leave the area, and all he got from the time he walked through the door at lunchtime until breakfast next morning was hassle. How was he supposed to play football under conditions like that?

There's other pressure, too. If you have a bad day on Saturday you and the rest of the world know all about it, because you read about it the next day in the Sunday papers.

Written off

It's all about opinions, I know, but I don't like reporters gratuitously slagging people off, and that was done while I was with Plymouth. I don't think anybody's got a right to do that. They can say that a player's had a good game or an absolute nightmare but not that he's a total waste of space and time, which has been said. Punters do not want to hear that, anyway. They want a report on the game.

Too many reporters and commentators on the television are trying to be coaches. I heard one on the television the other day saying that when A passed to B and it didn't come off he should have tried doing something else. I don't think that's right. That's coaching, not commentating. I know they watch a lot of football but I don't like it.

It's no good having a go at pressmen, even though I think reporters should report on games rather than offer opinions. People want to know what's happened not what someone thinks about what's happened. A lot of pressmen make comments which shouldn't be made.

You should know in yourself when you're playing badly and that all boils down to lack of confidence. It can get on top of you if the papers are having a go at you as well.

You've got to come out of it. I've been knocked in print but it doesn't affect me, although sometimes when I've had a bad game I purposely don't buy the papers.

I've had some terrible games but scored a goal or two and got eight out of ten or four stars out of five in the paper's ratings the next day and I've thought :"Was he really at the same game?" and I've played reasonably well and haven't scored and got five out of ten or two stars and wondered how the hell that guy's come to that conclusion.

Half the time, newspaper people don't know what they are talking about because they haven't played the game. There's very few that I dislike, though - I get on very well with most of them. Some make comments about the game without really reporting on the game and you might see things totally differently to them. I've read a report on some games and, like I say, I wonder if they've actually been at the same match. In one game I headed the ball straight at their goalkeeper and I read the next day that he pulled off a brilliant save to deny me.

At the end of the day, forwards are judged by scoring goals and creating chances and reporters are probably right in saying you only had a half-decent game if that doesn't happen.

But I do think that some of them don't know what they're talking about. No disrespect to women but I wouldn't read any report on a game written by a woman. I don't think it is right for a woman to report on football, especially professional football.

There are a few around, and to be fair to them they are probably quite good. But most men have actually played the game at some level. Football is a man's game, it's born and bred into you, and women reporting on it doesn't gel.

Grounds for concern

Reporters sometimes don't know the sort of conditions players have had to put up with before a match, either. I've never seen a place like Hartlepool in my life, although I'm talking years and years ago so it's probably changed now.

There was an old boiler in the corner and you had to light it to get the heating going for the water. When I played their with Sheffield Wednesday, Tony Toms lit the boiler and it just exploded because he'd forgotten to let the gas in slowly. Then one of the lads put his elbow through the wall, which was made of chipboard, and found himself looking through the hole in to the road outside. It didn't really put us in a good frame of mind for the match.

At Frickley Athletic, where I played for Rotherham in the FA Cup, their central-heating was a coal fire in the middle of the dressing room. A nice bit of psychology that, because they were used to the conditions and their opponents weren't. It was cold, the middle of winter and the ground was rock hard. They had showers though. Two of them. For 12 lads.

Maesteg, who I played against for Newport in the Welsh Cup, was in a valley with houses on all four sides. The pitch reminded me of a field, like our back yard is now, thick grass and divots all over the place. Unbelievable.

The away dressing room at Newport wasn't too clever either. It was very small and there was a hole in the wall which you had to climb through for the showers. Not the best place in the world.

At the other end of the scale, I've played at some good grounds. New York was brilliant. The Americans had some wild ideas. When I was at Dallas, we played Manchester United and, instead of trotting out from the tunnel, we rode on to the pitch on horses wearing stetsons which we gave to their players as gifts. The stetsons, not the horses. The crowd used to shout your name as you rode out. But the club stopped that caper because Jimmy Ryan, who is now manager at Luton, came in and his horse started bucking wildly, throwing him off. He did his groin and couldn't play. He'd only been there about two weeks.

Another time, we were lined up ready to kick-off before the match but there was no ball. Then this chap carrying the ball parachuted down into the centre circle but landed too heavily and broke his back. He was eventually stretchered off and the game was inevitably delayed. They stopped that escapade as well.

The most bizarre thing was when Tampa Bay Rowdies came on before a match all riding on elephants. Rodney Marsh doing his impersonation of a mahout! I also played in one game when the team came out in a stagecoach and in New York we played on a baseball pitch which was covered in the most lovely green turf unfortunately surrounded by a diamond of sand.

It must have been hell being a spectator in America though. There were kids wandering round trying to sell you about 20 different things: hot-dogs, hamburgers, pennants, the works. I watched one game and just spent the whole of the 90 minutes telling these kids to get out of the way.

Dallas also had a guy called Crazy Larry, who was paid $50,000 a year just to go round the ground banging a drum to whip everyone up. I didn't like America because the razzmatazz was way over the top. It's not sport.

But the Americans do things well and the financial side of things is really sound. The 1994 World Cup is in safe hands, but they were just a little bit too overbearing for me.

They're lacking in a bit of sense of humour, mind you. When I was in America I was playing with a fellow called Roy Turner, who was an apprentice at Everton, and he was sent off in my first match. It happened like this. I came on as substitute with 20 minutes to go and the first thing that happened was that I was fouled. Roy said: "Come on ref, get you effing book out." So he said: "Right, I will" and showed Roy the yellow card. Roy said: "I'll twist. " The ref pulled out the red card and sent him off!

Anfield is probably not the best stadium in the country but the atmosphere is the special thing. It's unbelievable and it's down to the people. Everton is the same, a lovely ground to play at. They're both super surfaces, you can't argue with that, but I think the atmosphere that is created by the crowds is what makes them that extra little bit special. It's love and need. They love football and they need it.

Of course the atmosphere affects people, especially the opposition, and there are basically two ways it affects them. You can hear the crowd, virtually feel it when you go out, and freeze. Or you can respond positively to it. That's the way it gets me, although it's difficult to describe accurately the exact feeling I get.

Prized possesion: My treasured Golden Boot.

Ton up: My 100th Football League goal for Argyle, against Blackburn, November 5, 1988.

Fans favourite: Argyle Player-of-the-Year, 1985.

Ready to strike: Another goal, against West Bromwich Albion this time.

Treble top: Plymouth Player-of-the-Year, 1989.

Pick that one out: Oldham Athletic fail to stop me scoring.

On the spot: Baffled by a rare penalty miss against Shrewsbury.

Unlucky 13: With Dave Smith on one of the rare occasions I was Argyle sub.

9

RETURN TICKET TO PLYMOUTH

I INITIALLY signed for Plymouth from Newport because I was very impressed with the manager Bobby Moncur. We spoke very openly to each other and he told me he was thinking of playing me up front alongside John Sims, who I was a big admirer of, with Gordon Staniforth out wide. I went back to Newport to sort a few things out and when I came back John had gone to Torquay. It was a bit of a shock, finding that out.

I started playing up front with Gordon Staniforth and I didn't have the best of starts. I wasn't scoring. Then Bobby Moncur and the board parted company and they brought Johnny Hore in, a move which I think astounded a lot of people.

Argyle's run to the 1984 FA Cup semi-final perked me - and everyone else - up and I started the following year reasonably well. I was on eight goals when Dave Smith came to replace John Hore and I just carried on from there in the same vein. I ended on 33 goals, won the player of the season award and began a great understanding with the new manager.

But my contract was up at the end of the season, my wife was pregnant and wanted to move back nearer her family in Sheffield, and Plymouth were not offering me the right terms. What they were offering me insulted my intelligence.

Even right up to the last game of the season, when we played Millwall away, they didn't come up with what I wanted and I'd asked for a new contract months before, just after Christmas. I'd never have left if they had said yes then.

It came to the summer and out of the blue Dave Smith phoned me and said : "They'll give you what you want.'' But my mind was already made up. I'd spoken to a few clubs and the only ones that were really interested were Middlesbrough and Rotherham. I signed for Rotherham because there was no hesitation with the fee or my personal terms and my wife was happy.

I had a good season after a poor start in Yorkshire and then fell out with the manager, Norman Hunter, who relegated me to the reserves. I played three or four games for the reserves and, just before the transfer deadline, I had nine clubs who wanted me on loan for the last three months of the season.

A bit of a hero

Chesterfield were doing quite well and asked me to sign for them, £1,000 cash in hand. I asked for assurances in writing and was told that they couldn't do that because it would all be in readies. Later that day, they phoned me up at midnight and said they desperately needed a goalscorer and were prepared to pay me £100-a-goal plus the original £1,000. I again asked for it in writing and they said they couldn't do that.

Port Vale came in with a similar offer, and Cardiff and Blackpool and two or three others contacted me. Then Chesterfield came back, upping their offer to £1,000 and £200-a-goal. All this happened before Plymouth had even come in for me, two or three days before I'd even heard from Dave Smith. Then he rang me and asked me if I fancied coming back to Plymouth on loan. He said he needed someone to give them that extra edge in their final drive for promotion to the Second Division. I told him what had been happening. Then Chesterfield phoned up and increased their offer to £1,000 and £300-a-goal. I told them I was going to see Dave Smith.

Smithy met me at Frankly Services on the M5 and we spoke for half-an-hour. I told him what other clubs had been offering me and he said he couldn't match that but would take care of me in one or two other ways. To be honest, he didn't have to because I'd made up my mind to sign anyway.

Looking at it coldly, Plymouth were playing well and in with a chance of promotion. I was going to play nine games for Plymouth and if they went up I would get the money for getting promoted and my expenses, plus they would look after me. And if I could score a few goals and help them win promotion, I'd be a bit of a hero.

When I returned from the meeting, Chesterfield rang again and said to forget about the goals, they would give me £2,000 in my hand. I asked for it in writing again and when they said they couldn't, I told them to forget it. At the end of the day, I made the right decision. If I had not come back to Plymouth on loan, I never would have joined them later. Everything stemmed from those ten goals in nine games.

If Chesterfield had come back to me and given me assurances in writing then I might have signed for them. But coming to Plymouth wasn't a purely financial decision.

I got exactly the same bonuses as the other players, but they got theirs pro rata. They'd played 40-odd games and I'd played nine and I didn't get whacked for tax like them. One of my team-mates moaned: "You got £250 more than me and I played all bloody season" because he got whacked for tax and I didn't.

I can remember clear as day the nine games I played for Plymouth when I came back from Rotherham on loan. I nearly didn't play in the first match because the forms weren't through in time, but the game was postponed which enabled me to play.

And I scored twice against Rotherham, the second of which Dave Smith said afterwards not many people would have got. Steve Cooper screwed his shot wide and I scored only because I saw him shape up and anticipated he'd miss.

There was one bad memory, too. When Wigan beat us 3-0, I went round to the pub to ring my wife up. When I walked in I heard someone say: "There's one of those Argyle bastards. Our season's over now thanks to them." I just turned around and walked out. I don't even think they'd been at the game.

I had a great three months. I stayed with Leigh Cooper and his wife Karen, which was better than digs. It was really good of them to let me stay there. I also found a total change of atmosphere at the club compared to the first time I'd been there.

I don't know whether Dave Smith had done it deliberately but he had assembled a group of people who got on well with each other, which simply wasn't the case before. People like John Clayton, Kevin Summerfield, John Matthews and Gerry McElhinney had all been about a bit and knew the scene, and it was a different place. I could easily understand how they were doing so well.

I got slaughtered when I returned to Rotherham after the loan because of the two goals I'd scored against them. They claimed there was supposed to be a gentlemen's agreement between me and Rotherham that I wouldn't play, but that's a load of rubbish because it's the two clubs which are supposed to come to any such arrangement, and they hadn't.

When I was back at Rotherham after my loan spell with Plymouth, Dave Smith was always in contact with me, asking me how I was and telling me who he was looking at, but he never said he wanted me back. I asked him whether he'd spoken to Norman Hunter and he said: "Yes and no" whatever that meant. Then all of a sudden he made a bid for me. I heard about it, asked Dave Smith if it was true, and went to see Norman Hunter who said it was up to me whether I wanted to stay or not. I returned to Plymouth and Norman got the sack halfway through the season. I've taken half-calculated risks which have come off because I knew who I was dealing with.

It wasn't up to me whether I'd come back to Plymouth and I wouldn't have been allowed to come back if it had been up to half the board of directors. Their philosophy was that they didn't want me back because I'd left originally. One or two thought I'd made a financial killing, but I hadn't.

The board didn't know I was going to sign again. When I arrived at the ground, Dave Smith told me he hadn't said a word to them and he was just going to take me into the boardroom in the middle of their meeting. He strolled in and said: "Good afternoon, gentlemen. How are you? I've got someone here to see you." I walked in on cue and said hello to looks of amazement. When they'd established I was signing, Dave Smith said: "Come on, they're in the middle of a meeting" and we left. Typical Smithy.

Second time around

When I came back to Plymouth in 1986 people warned me: "It's not going to be the same second time around" and they were right. It actually worked out a lot better for me. I was in a house within six weeks, unlike when I'd moved from Newport; I had my family down straight away and my kids settled in school, which also helped.

There was never an annual night out for the players when I first came to Plymouth. It wasn't even thought about until Leigh Cooper and I mentioned that maybe we should have one. At most of the clubs I've been, the players have their own Christmas party together and they take their wives and girlfriends out as well, which never happened at Plymouth. Now they put a fiver-a-week away each and take the wives out for a big do at the Holiday Inn.

The last three or four Christmas dos in Plymouth have been exceptional. I don't know what people must have thought if they saw twenty full-grown men, Plymouth Argyle's professional footballers, staggering down Cornwall Street in the middle of the afternoon though.

We had some great players' dos at Sheffield Wednesday, too. I'll always remember one when Mick Prendergast had left his car parked, because he knew he wouldn't be able to drive it home, but he went back to it just to check that it was locked. When he returned, a couple of coppers approached him. He had no intention of driving, he was far too drunk, and he told them: "You take the keys" but it looked nasty. Hughie Dowd went over to them shouting: "You bastards. Why don't you go out and pull some rapists or burglars?" and the rest of us were just laughing our heads off. It's a good job the coppers realised it was a social and told

Mick to shut the car up and go away. A lot of policemen aren't like that nowadays, I'm afraid.

The first two years that I was at Plymouth were totally different from the time after I came back. Second time around players all went out together, whereas before it was all little cliques of two or three together. The players all got on well socially when I came back. Having the three testimonial years for John Uzzell, Kevin Hodges and Leigh Cooper also made a difference I think. Everybody went into bat for everybody else.

You either hit it off with a manager or you don't and with Dave Smith it was as if I'd known him all my life. He just let me play football. He didn't put any restrictions on me and that was good as far as I was concerned. I'd had defensive duties under Bobby Moncur and Johnny Hore which I couldn't handle because I'd never done it before. Dave Smith took the restrictions away from me and I started enjoying my football again and scoring goals.

He was totally different from what I'd been used to and, at times, very, very eccentric.

When he came to Plymouth, he introduced the long-ball game and said: "This is the new way of football, everyone's going to be doing it this way soon." I hoped they wouldn't, but he was at least half-right because the long-ball game certainly came to the fore then.

I felt he lost his way a bit at Plymouth which is why he left for Dundee. I don't know whether it was loss of love for the club or that he'd simply felt he had gone as far as he could with the players that he had.

I don't really feel that he had the right players to play the system he was playing. If you're going to play that way you've got to have a couple of big lads up front and strong midfield runners to get on the end of balls, which we didn't really have. We had more of a footballing side. But it worked for a time.

Leading from the front

There came a time when Dave Smith and his coach, Stewart Houston didn't feel they had anyone strong enough to be captain with the

Plymouth team we had. One day they pulled me aside after training and told me they'd been thinking about making me captain.

I said: "To be honest gaffer, if I was manager I'd have a defender or midfielder as captain, because they can see more of the play better. But if you want me to do it, I'll do it."

A couple of weeks went by, then Gerry McElhinney, who was captain, was injured or left out - I can't remember which - and Dave Smith asked me to take over.

I totally enjoyed being captain although I know a lot of people don't like the responsibility of captaincy because of the commitments it involves.

To my mind, being a captain of a football club is not simply about leading a side on to the football field. People should be able to look at the captain and say: "He's smartly dressed; he's well presented; he does a lot of work for charity." Whatever.

Everything comes through you when you are captain. I had to delegate who did which presentations or charity work, although a lot of times there were certain things, which, because of other commitments, we simply could not do.

As captain, you're not only projecting yourself, you're projecting the image of the club, which I hope I did well. I certainly enjoyed every minute of it.

There might have been a little bit of resentment when I was appointed captain at Plymouth. But it was a bit easier because I didn't have any what you would call close friends, except Leigh Cooper.

A lot of the media attention has always been on me because I have done well and scored goals consistently and I think that might have brought about a touch of jealously, though not so much towards the end of my Home Park career.

It came to a head when I wasn't scoring towards the end of the 1987/88 season, because no-one can say a word when you are playing well and scoring goals. One or two people were saying I was only in the side because I was captain and I ought to be left out because I wasn't producing.

Possibly the manager should have left me out for a couple of games. I might have come back refreshed and scored a couple of goals and things would have been different. It went on too long.

On the pitch, you can get away with a hell of a lot more as captain. Referees will tell you that if they need to speak to a player, they'll speak through you and they also know that you're trying to speak to them about certain incidents on behalf of other players.

As long as you're not abusive and don't wave your arms around, the referee will respond. It's very rarely you'll ever see a captain booked for anything other than a bad tackle.

10

SCENES BEHIND THE SCENES

EVEN MY wife, who knows a lot about the game, cannot believe how much power a manager has got. He can ruin your life totally if he wants to exert all his power over you. But fortunately all of the managers I have played under, except for Jack Charlton and Norman Hunter, have been very reasonable with me and haven't tried to use their power unnecessarily.

Managers can have you in for training at ten in the morning, two in the afternoon and six at night every day if they want to, and take you on every away trip without playing you if they were really trying to make your life a misery. They don't gain anything by doing it but they can do anything they want as long as it's in your contract and in the club rules. In one way it's good because players should realise who's in charge, but in another way it's bad because abused power can totally demoralise the player concerned.

At Newport once, five or six players were banished from the dressing room, told they were the pits of the club and that they were not wanted. They were made to train on their own and get changed in their own dressing room. Managers can lose respect from players when they don't appear to have power, but sometimes they can lose respect just as easily when they overuse their power.

I've known managers phone up other managers and ask about certain players and they've been told not to touch him because he's a bad so-and-so or whatever. Next thing, the manager who has given this advice has gone out and signed the player. Sometimes the power goes to their heads. Certain clubs use private detectives to go into some background about players they want to buy. I think that's taking things a bit too far.

When I fell out with Norman Hunter at Rotherham, he told me to train with the kids, do my own training, and he played me in the reserves. It was in his interests to keep me fit so he could sell me, if that was what he wanted, but I don't think he should have done what he did. It's no good playing a player in the reserves just because he's on the transfer list. If he's good enough he should be in the first-team, where he's got to do the business because that's the only way he'll get a move.

Putting yourself in the shop window is not the same as playing for a move. Playing for a move is where a player, under contract and wanting a transfer, is not being allowed to move. He'll do just enough in a game to justify his selection and attract the attention of other clubs without putting himself out too much, hoping the manager will lose patience and say: "That's it, off you go." It happens less often now because of the influence that the Professional Footballers Association has on the game. They can mediate in disputes and advise their members.

Myth and motivation

Different managers do different things before games. At Argyle, Ken Brown was always in and out of the dressing room. He'd come in and then go missing for about 20 minutes while everyone did their warm-ups. He liked to go to the referee's room, then he'd come back and have a little word. Dave Smith would come in at 2 pm if he hadn't named the side and then all of a sudden he'd go and have a drink in the Green Room and come back about a quarter-of-an-hour before kick-off.

Most managers that I've known sit you down and go through some pretty general stuff from about 2 pm onwards. Everyone wants to know what the opposition line-up is because you've always got a report on the team you're playing, how they work their free-kicks and corners, that sort of thing. Ken Brown would talk to individual players. He didn't sit us all down and talk to us generally, trying to motivate us. In the Littlewood's Cup game against Arsenal last season, he said that we'd got it all to do and that we should just go out and enjoy ourselves and try and score a few goals. We didn't do either, losing 6-1.

I think there's a myth about people motivating you. Managers don't do a lot before a game besides running through the opposition's set-pieces. The actual motivation is down to yourself really. People might describe a manager as a great motivator, but what they mean is that he's good at man-management.

Every player is different and and managers gee-up players differently. But they don't do it just before a game, they do it on the Thursday or Friday beforehand. They tell you during training what is expected of you on Saturday.

I've never known a manager come up and try to really get you going. They encourage you and say: "Do what you're good at" or something along those lines. I don't know what motivating is and I don't think Ken Brown did either. He never went round geeing people up.

Dave Smith, on the other hand, used to hit people. He would go round the dressing room and hit you on the arms or the back shouting: "Come on, come on." He's a great believer in the American way of doing things. Then he'd stand in the tunnel and wish you all the best as you went on. Most managers don't do that. They leave the dressing room and just go straight upstairs to the stand.

A lot of people get geed-up by different things. If a manager has a go at a player, the player might react in one of three ways. He might just drop his head because of the criticism; he might have a go back; or he might make up his mind to go out and prove the manager wrong. You can't have a go at some players at all. You've got to praise them all the time to get them going. Obviously everyone likes praise, but when I was younger I needed someone to have a go at me to get me going.

When he was at Plymouth, Ken Brown rarely said anything to me at all, or to any of the senior players. I've been in the game 18 years and I know what it is all about. If the manager or the coaches ever said anything to me it was just to keep everything going.

David Kemp is very fond of using a board in the dressing room before the match. He uses it to show the players all the opposition's free-kicks and corners and to actually write down the name of the player that everyone is supposed to be picking up at each of them.

About three-quarters of the Argyle players last season would shout to themselves as they were going out onto the pitch. Kenny Brown was one. He'd shout really aggressively to get himself and everyone else going. It's a way of getting your mind right for the task in hand, although it doesn't always work that way.

I can see their thinking. The bigger the game, the more tense you get and any way of working the tension out of your system is a good idea.

Generally, Ken Brown used to tell his players: "Just go out and play football." That's all very well, but Liverpool don't do that and they're the best in the country. We needed David Kemp's introduction of a pattern of play because there were players on the pitch on a Saturday afternoon who didn't know what they were supposed to be doing.

Ken Brown, though, is a real players' manager. He treats you like a man, not a boy, which I believe is important. He lets you have a drink and at Plymouth he even came out with the players to social functions, which is quite unusual for a manager.

He's also not the type to say that you've got to be in by midnight every night. He respects footballers as professionals and as professionals we know there are certain things you don't do on certain days. No visiting pubs 48 hours before a match, for instance.

He brought a new sense of awareness to the Plymouth players. He got us looking very smart, like a team. He let us have a laugh and a joke in training, which meant that his coach, Martin Harvey and physiotherapist, Malcolm Musgrove sometimes had a very difficult job. Some of the lads can be a bit of a handful when they are together and in certain moods.

I can understand why he was so well liked, both by the people at Norwich and the people at Plymouth. There were times when he never stopped laughing, always had a smile on his face.

His coaching abilities were something else. I've never known someone employ such a variety of five-a-side games. I enjoyed working with him and I believe Ken Brown played the way professionals like to play - pure, patient football.

Martin Harvey and Malcolm Musgrove thought the world of him when he came down here. Martin played at the very highest level of the game and was a very good coach, although in the six years I knew him I must have called him every name under the sun! People should have seen the pair of them in five-a-side matches in training, Malcolm says he's 50, must be nearer 70, and can't run or see but, I tell you what, he can cross the ball, pass the ball and do the simple things very well.

Everyone talks about the manager. Coaches and physiotherapists hardly get a mention. Martin and Malcolm are not only very good coaches but also very nice people and they get a lot of respect from players because players know that they know what they are talking about.

The worst thing in the world for a manager is that he's not out there, playing. He can't do a thing after he's said his piece just before 3 pm. It's down to the players then. At half-time, he has to do what he thinks best and it doesn't always depend on the score after 45 minutes.

Sometimes we've been losing and the manager has just said that we're still in the game and just to keep doing the right things; other times we've been playing quite well and winning but we've been absolutely slaughtered. What he's saying then is that: "This one could slip away from you if you're not careful." He's having a go simply to get you on your guard and make sure your standards don't drop. That's especially the case if the game's 0-0 and you should have scored three or four because the other team is still in with an even chance.

Ken Brown rarely used to single out individuals for a roasting, but Dave Smith would and Len Ashurst would absolutely slaughter players individually. He'd pick on someone in front of everyone and pull them apart.

David Kemp did pick on individuals, but not to bawl them out. He'd have a little bit of paper in his hands, on which he's made notes, and he'd refer to them, pointing out one or two things. Then he'd say "Get on with it." The whole process would only take two or three minutes.

Squaring up

The real rows are always at full-time because you very rarely say anything back to the manager at half-time. He's trying to keep you going at half-time and you respect that, but at full-time the game has gone by. If it's also gone badly, that is when the arguments break out.

Len Ashurst would always have a go at the midfielders and defenders, hardly ever the forwards. Forwards change a game by scoring or creating goals and he would never tell off a forward for missing a chance because at least he was in there having a go. The only time he roasted me or any of the forwards was for not working.

I've seen players at Sheffield Wednesday and Newport come off at full-time, take off their shirts and throw them at the manager before walking into the dressing room. I remember Dave Cusack slinging his boot at Len Ashurst at Sheffield. We'd drawn 1-1 against Swindon but hadn't played very well and should have been beaten easily. Len blamed Dave for not pushing up and dropping off properly and was having a right go at him. Dave snapped and threw his boot at Len.

Len got the sack soon afterwards and was probably having a go at Dave because he was under pressure himself. Managers are frequently under pressure and sometimes some of the things they come out with are not really in character. He might think something but hold back from actually saying it when he's not under pressure. But when the chips are down, he might have a go.

Players sometimes have a go at each other. The reason for that is total frustration, often because there's a team-mate out on the park who simply doesn't want to know. The resentment builds up during a game if a player isn't doing what another player thinks he ought to be doing. The rows between players aren't personal. Nine times out of ten you don't have a go at someone because you don't like him as a person. It's simply a disagreement about football.

It gets overheated and if you've got a short wire, you blow up, although you might as well talk to a brick wall most of the time for all the good it does you.

Most of the incidents I've been involved in or known about have blown over inside a week or two, though. It's totally stupid for players to carry a grudge against each other because, in this game, it will crucify you.

I've heard a lot of stories about dressing room bust-ups with opposition players but I've never really been involved in any. I've heard stories about players fighting with managers but I've never really seen that either.

A former Torquay player told me himself how he'd had Bruce Rioch by the throat in his office when Rioch was manager at Plainmoor. They had an argument about money or something and the verbals led to a bit of a set-to. I don't think the player played again, for Torquay or anyone else.

Players are too professional to let their on-field rivalries spill over into the players' lounges after a game. I've never seen physical or verbal intimidation which has been present on the field continue afterwards. After all it's just a game of football and that's what you're there for. You'd soon be on your way if the manager or the club found out about any incident afterwards. It's professional suicide. There have been incidents immediately after matches, though I've never seen animosity spill out into the bar afterwards. When Wimbledon played at Plymouth and the match was abandoned, I saw one of their players have a go at one of our lads in the tunnel.

I've had a go at team-mates in the dressing room myself. Last season when Sheffield United played at Argyle, I had a go at David Byrne, who had come on as substitute. The match, which ended 0-0, was very frustrating for both sides and Budgie was bawling and shouting, like he does sometimes. I asked him if he was having a go and he turned round and said words to the affect that I should have been taken off. I think that is unacceptable for one player to say to another. It doesn't do anyone any good at all.

The situation went on all through the game. Later, Carl Bradshaw, who was playing for Sheffield, asked me: "Why was your 12 having a go at you for nothing?" That was his reaction and my reaction as well. Dave didn't think that and expressed it in a typical way. Afterwards, he wouldn't even talk to me. I grabbed him and said: "If you've got anything to say about me, say it to my face." And he replied: "I'm only saying what the gaffer was saying."

In the bath, he blanked me again. When I approached him he just walked away, and I asked him why he couldn't face me. He threatened me and I told him anytime he wanted to try it he was welcome. I think it was just frustration. The same night we went for a beer in town at The Bank and we had a decent night out. We're grown men and the incident was forgotten. We're still quite friendly and the incident didn't affect things on the field. If I was in the box and he was in a position to give it to me, he gave it. There's certain players who wouldn't have reacted like that, but he's not one of them. Maybe I reacted a little strongly but I don't think you should say to someone: "You were rubbish, you should have been taken off."

Dave has been about a bit and he's basically a good professional, not the sort of player to hold a grudge, and there has been no lasting animosity. That's often the case. When I first came to Plymouth, though, I had a go at other players and they would blank me for the rest of the game.

When I was at Newport, I had a go at another player, one of my team-mates. Steve Lowndes told me to eff off all the way to the dressing room and we went for each other. But we were split up and that was that.

A coach who I respect, and who is now a good friend, once offered to take me outside to sort out a few things. Graham Davies and Dave Bruton were team-mates at Newport but that didn't stop them throwing punches after a game. The flare-up happened because one of them thought the other shouldn't be playing and told the other so.

You've got to get on with it. It's the same as someone kicking you in training. At Plymouth, Torquay or any other club, everyone does not like everyone else at club. It is being unprofessional, though, if you go out for a match and won't pass the ball to someone because you don't get on with him.

Colin Addison came to the Newport and he knew people weren't getting on very well. One of the first things he did was to sit everyone down in the dressing room and say: "It doesn't matter whether you don't like him or he doesn't like you, whether he's been married five times or whether he's a homosexual. At 3 pm on Saturday, you're all fighting for each other, to win the game, to win your bonus. That's what you do from now on." He was right, and that is generally what happens.

Aggression and intimidation

If you have got twenty professionals at a club, not everyone is going to like each other, but you've still got to go out and do the business on a Saturday afternoon. I've never not passed to someone because I don't like him and don't want him to get the glory of scoring. If he's in a better position than me and that pass gives him the chance of securing a win or a draw, then you've got to do it. You're not going out with him afterwards but you still get your money because you've acted in a professional way.

In any team, however successful, you don't get on with everyone. You can't. There have been players in teams that I've played for who would not go out for a drink with you because they disliked you so much. But you get on with it on the field because you are a professional. Colin Addison had the right attitude. You play for each other, because when you win you're all successful and you all pick up the same win bonus. That's true, that's the way it is.

Players are very aggressive to each other and that aggression intensifies during a match. Say I was having a go at Sean McCarthy last season. I didn't go up to him and say: "Well look here Sean, you should have controlled that ball a little bit better and tried to play me in." I say: "Why the effing hell didn't you pass the ball?" That goes on, that's acceptable. I didn't walk up to Adrian Burrows and say: "Excuse me old chap, but I think you should have put that ball in the back row of the stand." I said: "Why the effing hell didn't you clear the stand with that?" The reaction in those circumstances will always be the same: "Yeah, sorry" because he knows. It's a form of shorthand. Professional football is played largely by the working classes, you're among men, and every third word is an expletive. It's okay as long as it's not at the top of your voice.

Swearing goes on but I can honestly say I've never heard a player swear at a fan. I've seen them make gestures - I've made one or two myself - but I can't remember an incident when a player has sworn at a spectator.

An opposition player can say what he wants to me during a game. He can tell me he's going to break my leg if he likes. That goes on; it's called intimidation. When I was at Liverpool, one of my earliest memories was hearing one of the opposition tell David Fairclough that he'd get his leg broken if he came within a yard of him. Certain clubs have been doing that sort of thing for years and it serves it's purpose of putting you off your game if you let it get to you. You can't stop it, either.

I've never had anybody make derogatory remarks to me about my wife or kids, or my parents, though. Nothing personal. That isn't acceptable and I don't know any manager who would endorse that if he knew it was going on.

I always remember once at Liverpool when they were playing Arsenal, Tommy Smith was standing by the tunnel when George Armstrong came out for warm-up. Tom said: "'Geordie, I'm going to kick you today." Armstrong replied: "I know you are Tom, but you'll have to catch me first."

That's just banter though, and that goes on during matches as well. Dave Smith used to have this bee in his bonnet about me and Dave Cusack, who I know well. I'd come in after a game and Smithy said: "What were you doing talking on the halfway line, having a chat in the middle of the game?" I said I was just asking him how his wife was. He said: "What about the game?" I said "The ball was right down the other end." It's nice coming up against someone you know, you can find out how they're going, how their wife and kids are.

At the other end of the scale, there's the other types, nasty pieces of work who go straight through you the first time the ball is played up to you. You have a go at him and he tells you that that's what he's been told to do and that's what he intends doing at every opportunity. When Plymouth played Cardiff in the Littlewood's Cup last season, I could have taken the kid to the toilet with me, he was that close all the time. He just followed me everywhere for 90 minutes. I know a lot of managers who will tell their players to do anything they can to knock you off your game.

John Aldridge broke a fellow's jaw when he was playing in a Cardiff/ Newport derby match. He had been punched off the ball and the next time he went for a header, he caught up with the person responsible. Everyone knew he'd done it and why, but the referee didn't see it.

I don't think there's a lot in today's game that is out of order. What Paul Davis did to Glenn Cockerill was out of order, because he actually broke his cheekbone. You can punch someone and nothing happens because it is just a punch, there's no damage done. I don't think Davis would have had such a long ban if or there would have been such a fuss if Cockerill had just gone down and got up. But a big deal was made of it because his cheekbone was broken and Davis's punch was shown repeatedly on television.

11

SUCCESS

COLIN ADDISON, who I enjoyed playing under at Newport, was great for one-liners and he once said: "Most players never have much success in their careers but there are always some triumphs worth celebrating."

Success comes very early to some people and a few players enjoy a lot of success but a lot never win a trophy or a medal in their entire career. For me, the 1980/81 European Cup-Winners Cup run with Newport, the 1983/84 FA Cup run with Plymouth, and two promotion seasons with the same two clubs have been my personal successes. And I would never have remembered them with so much affection if I hadn't celebrated them.

At Newport, we won promotion from the Fourth Division in 1980 and then we won the Welsh Cup two weeks later. One of the lads went home after the cup win as if it was normal game or a mundane training session. I couldn't believe it. We had five or six crates of champagne to get through!

Home Park to Villa Park

The run to the FA Cup semi-final with Plymouth just went on and on.

It was like our own cup final every time a cup match came around because we weren't having a good season in the Third Division by any stretch of the imagination. In fact, we nearly got relegated.

The only difficult game we had before the semi-final against Watford at Villa Park was at West Bromwich Albion in the fifth round. Derby were relegated from the Second Division that season and were on a downer and the rest of the draw - Southend, Barking, Newport and Darlington were the other sides we played - gave us just what we needed.

The memories of the semi-final all blend into one another. First of all, the crowd was unbelievable, Westcountry fans at their best. I thought we were the better side in the first-half, even though Watford scored the only goal of the game. We played some very attractive football and it was one of the few games that season when I didn't shout at anybody because the balls played up to the front were way above our normal Third Division class.

Gordon Staniforth and I had a lot of possession and there was always someone spare to lay the ball off to. You know things are going well for you when you are getting plenty of touches and I was getting plenty. The second-half was a different story. Maybe they were a little bit stronger, but we had chances right up until the death when Kevin Hodges' shot went just wide.

I had a couple of shots at goal, one of which flew over the bar and another which I badly miscued from a long way out. But the team as a whole did not really have a lot of chances. At the end of the day, I think it would have been a fairer result if we'd come away with a 1-1 draw instead of a 1-0 defeat. Their goal came early in the game and, besides picking the ball out of the net, Geoff Crudgington did not have a lot to do, maybe just make one or two saves. I think we could have won, but that's the way it goes.

Leigh Cooper was very upset after the game because his error led to their goal. He did not feel he'd lost the game for us but he was still aware that it was his mistake in giving the ball away to John Barnes - who crossed for George Reilly to head in - that let them in. He still thinks he let the lads down, which is ridiculous because he didn't. Everyone acquitted themselves as best they could.

Leigh was upset because Plymouth Argyle has been his life and he was the captain. The manager, John Hore treated Leigh with respect and even now you will never hear Leigh say a bad word about John Hore, whatever others may think of him.

At the time, the semi-final meant everything to everyone but I can be level-headed about it now because it is all in the past. Playing in an FA Cup final is the one thing that every player wants to achieve. Some of the best players have never been to Wembley and I would have liked to have had the chance, but it never happened. I never played in the First Division but I never worried about that either because it never happened.

Coaches tell you: "Go out, play your hardest for 90 minutes and don't come back into the dressing room and say 'If I'd done this, we'd have scored' or 'If I hadn't done this, they wouldn't have got their goal.' " It's the same with the FA Cup semi-final. You play it; you lose; you remember it as clear as day for a couple of weeks; and then you forget it. It has happened, it's all over.

In the cup, we played ever so well in every game, even the semi-final against Watford; in the league we were having a rough time and were in danger of relegation to the Fourth Division for the first time in the club's history. Thankfully, there was a good positive reaction to the semi-final which had a beneficial affect on our league form.

Because we had played so well and thought that we'd deserved to get through against Watford, or at least to get a replay, we went from strength to strength. Gordon Staniforth got three goals in our final four league games, which kept us from being relegated, although the cracks were still there.

I nearly didn't make it as far as the third round, let alone Villa Park, after falling out with John Hore at Christmas.

What happened was this. John Hore left me out of the side a few weeks after the second round tie. I couldn't believe it. I was just starting to play well even though I wasn't scoring. I watched our home game against Exeter on Boxing Day from the stands, and left early when we were winning 2-0 because I had my in-laws down for Christmas and they needed me to drive them to the station. When I came back, it was 2-2. After the game the manager told me to report on duty for the next day's match against Newport at Somerton Park.

I was having my pre-match meal the following day when he questioned me about leaving early. I explained and we had a bit of a row which ended with him saying: "I don't want you involved now. You can get yourself fixed up with another club." So I fixed up a three-month loan back at Newport which I thought, because of what he had said, he would agree to. But when the club spoke to him, he said I wasn't for sale or loan. Next game, I played. It was very unsettling. And who did we beat in the next round of the cup? Newport! And I scored a last-minute penalty to earn Plymouth a replay, too.

When Plymouth appointed Johnny Hore what the club was crying out for was an established manager who knew the Third Division and the ins and outs of league football. Instead, they got someone from non-league.

I think Johnny Hore becoming Plymouth manager was like me going back to Liverpool as manager there. He'd been involved with the club for 20 years and I felt he was in awe of the place.

Ask him now and I bet he'll tell you he would have done things differently, but he couldn't impose himself at the time because of his inexperience.

He thought there were a lot of players in non-league football as good as those in the Third Division and he tried to bring through a lot of non-league players, people like Terry Pooley and Terry Journeaux. There was a lot of animosity because these players had already been through the system and failed to make the grade.

Without being disrespectful to him, he ran the club as a non-league club. I don't think the club was run as a professional club or he himself was professional enough to get us out of the bad situation we were in.

Although we got to the semi-final of the FA Cup under him, we didn't have a good season. Earlier the following season, we got stuffed 7-2 by Bolton, had a bit of a meeting afterwards and expected things to be done by Monday. But we did the same old thing we had been doing for months, playing head tennis.

We didn't do anything under John Hore that even attempted to change our poor form. We weren't a bad side but we had some very bad results and didn't benefit from the FA Cup run as we should have done until right at the death.

European excursions

My previous, and only other, taste of cup success came three seasons earlier when Newport qualified for the European Cup-Winners Cup by virtue of winning the Welsh Cup the previous year.

We played Crusaders, of Northern Ireland, in the first round, after winning the first leg at Newport 4-0. The second leg ended 0-0 and afterwards every one of their players was changed and ready before us and, as we came out of the dressing room, one of their number was ready to look after each of us on a one-to-one basis.

They took us to the bar, bought us a Guinness - which was like cream - got us a buffet meal, sat us down and generally looked after us. While all this was going on, the secretary was getting held up by a bloke with a sub-machine gun.

The people over there were superb, though. You can't believe how friendly they were, for all the shooting and bombings you hear about. They were in a different class.

Carl Zeiss Jena, the East German side who we played in the quarter-final, were hard working, like most east European sides. They played Rome in the first round and just out-worked and outran the Italians, who were prima donnas really, and we pulled the same trick on them.

We went to their place and they were expecting us to be a very easy touch, but they didn't get what they were expecting. They went 1-0 up, I got the equaliser, then it was 2-1 and I got a second, and we still felt we'd done nothing special.

In the home leg it was so much one-way traffic it was unbelievable but we got beaten 1-0. That's football I suppose. We played so well and had a lot of chances. I hit the bar and hit the post; John Aldridge had a couple of chances, one of which was cleared off the line and another which went just over.

We must have had about eight chances in the game and if just one had gone in we would have won on the away goals rule. But it wasn't to be. They scored once, against the run of play, and that was that. The defeat stuck in my memory and those of the other lads for a long time afterwards. They were drawn against Benfica in the next round. Imagine the time we would have had in Portugal!

The away trip for the first leg was an eye-opener. You can't begin to believe how the people in East Germany live. It was horrible. Our coach-drive from the airport was supposed to take three hours, which was bad enough, but it took more like five because we must have been stopped at 20 different checkpoints to have our passports checked by the military.

The military are the only ones with any money. We were on £15-a-day day expenses but we got four or five times that amount on the black market because everybody wanted English money. They had what they called a Euro-shop where you could get a £400 camera for less than £100 if you had English money.

We were there for three days and instead of having £45 we had nearer £200 which meant we had a great time because money was no object. A lot of the lads bought cameras with the famous Carl Zeiss lens.

When they came to our place, they were allowed a drive around Newport and that was it. They were permitted an hour after the game to do some shopping because they'd won. Under guard all the time. You don't realise how lucky you are to live in this country until you go over there and see how poorly they live.

For a week after the European Cup-Winners Cup defeat, I couldn't forget that night. We were in the same position in the league as Plymouth were during the FA Cup run - struggling. In midweek I played against Carl Zeiss Jena in a big European tie and the following Saturday I played for the reserves at Maesteg. What a come down! I knew I was going to be dropped after the Cup-Winners Cup match when the manager, Len Ashurst came in the following morning and said: "There are some players here who have got to stop living on reputations."

I scored one of the goals against Maesteg and played for the reserves again in midweek and then Len Ashurst pulled me in and asked me if I fancied playing on the right-hand side of midfield. He left out Steve Lowndes, despite the fact the first-team had just won 3-1, but that's how he worked. He was under the impression that certain players needed leaving out every now and again as a kick up the backside. I could read him. At the end of the day, the players he relied on let him down and he was sacked.

Success is what it's all about and when you get it you'd be a fool not to enjoy it. You've got to celebrate because it might never happen to you again. Everyone wants to know you when you are successful. I got a free taxi ride after Plymouth won promotion. I'd never had a single one before. The guy just said: "This is on me." I've had a few since, mind you.

On the up and up

Winning promotion to the Second Division with Plymouth in 1986 was another unbelievable experience, and merely being part of it - even though I was only at Home Park on loan - was brilliant. The celebrations lasted for a week afterwards! The team which won Plymouth promotion - Dave Smith's team - was probably the best we had for five or six years, and that side was only together for one season really.

We had a civic reception after we played Exeter in the Devon Bowl. We all piled on to a bus and were taken to the Civic Centre where we met the mayor. The open-top bus crashed into the Civic Centre because the bus driver came in at the wrong angle and had to reverse.

There were 5,000 people outside the Civic Centre. Unbelievable, the best night I've ever had. Total enjoyment. We went out for meal afterwards and everyone wanted to know you, to say well done and to ask me if I was coming back on a permanent transfer. It was always on the cards but never cut and dried until much later.

What swung it for Dave Smith was that I wasn't happy at Rotherham and Plymouth hadn't started the following season that well. During

Argyle's match at Cardiff, one of the players ran through on an open goal and fell over the ball. The crowd started shouting: "There's only one Tommy Tynan" and he signed me the next day. I always thought I was coming back though, deep down. It was just a question of when and how. In the end it was the right decision.

The official crowd capacity that was given out on the night that Argyle won promotion in 1986 against Bristol City was given out as 20,000 but everybody realised there were far more than 20,000 there. A club official came into the dressing room and said that there were nearer 25,000 in the ground and that everyone's crowd bonus would be calculated on that figure. The club could have been in trouble if anyone from outside had known about the numbers because the crowd limit had been set at 20,000.

We celebrated on that Tuesday night and the next day the players had agreed to go to the Brook Inn in Plympton for our celebration. We still had to play Darlington, but the gaffer had given us a couple of days off. At 12.30 pm we were sitting down, having a few drinks, when the local television station's camera crew walked in and said: "We heard you were having a party. This is going on telly tonight." They hadn't been near us all year, apart form the last few weeks of the season, and suddenly they wanted anything and everything to do with us.

An illustration of how much that success can affect spirits came after our last game of the season. We'd just played Darlington, beaten them 2-0 and the team stopped off at Birmingham on the way back for a few drinks. The players had a few more drinks on the coach and people got a little bit happy, including the manager, Dave Smith, and one of the players, Russell Coughlin. When they got to Exeter, Russ was a little bit drunk and Dave Smith started having a little go at him. All of a sudden Russ called him a baldy bastard, got him on the floor and bit his nose. The manager eventually went home shoeless because someone had thrown one of his shoes out of the coach window. These things come with success. People let themselves go, including managers.

Cornered: Watching Andy Rogers' corner kick take Argyle into the 1984 FA Cup semi-final.

Bagging the winner: Scoring the goal which put First Division West Brom out of the 84 cup.

Champagne time: Celebrating reaching the 84 FA Cup semi-final.

Tuned in: Waiting, with Leigh Cooper, to find out who we've got in the next round of the FA Cup.

Going for goal: Finding no way past Steve Terry in the 84 FA Cup semi-final at Villa Park.

Magic moment: Kenny Brown and I swamp Sean McCarthy after he scored against Everton in the 89 FA Cup.

Grounded: A chance missed in the 89 FA Cup replay against Everton at Goodison Park.

Outgunned: Arsenal defender David O'Leary beats me to the ball in a Littlewoods Cup tie.

12

ALL IN THE FAMILY

MY KIDS never miss out on anything. Footballers have a lot of time on their hands and because of that Thomas, who doesn't go to school yet, sees me every day for eight or nine hours a day. But you can miss out on seeing your kids altogether when you're travelling, because they are at school when you leave and in bed when you get home again. Overall, the kids are lucky. I'm always here when Jordanna comes home from school and she sees more of me than some of her school friends see of their fathers.

I find it quite easy being a father, to be quite honest. The kids do wind you up now and again and Saturday at 10 am is not the greatest time in the world to throw a temper tantrum, if any time is a good time to throw a tantrum.

Saturdays generally fly by for me. I get up at 10 am, have some breakfast, watch a bit of telly, play with the kids, have a bath and get ready. All of a sudden it's 1 pm and I'm getting ready to play football. Sometimes the kids help actually. Having a play and a muck about with them can help take the tension out of things.

At the moment, they are going through a stage when they want to be at every game. Jordanna loves them, not so much for the game but for meeting the kids of the other players, who she can play with. It's nice when your family comes with you because they want to come with you - not because you've forced them - and they enjoy it. And, of course, their mum will never miss a game.

Tammy went through a stage when she was getting teased at school. People would say to her that she thought she was better than her schoolmates just because she is Tommy Tynan's daughter, which is untrue and totally unfair.

The kids don't resent their dad being famous. Jordanna gets a bit of teasing from the lads at her school if we get beaten. She's been upset at times but mostly it's alright. Thomas doesn't realise what's happening anyway. Keeley loves it and never wants to stop going to games.

A woman's touch

A lot of wives go to games only to watch their husbands. I wish that was the case with mine, but it isn't! She goes to watch the football. She always has done, ever since she was twelve or thirteen. She's interested in football. The first thing she'll say after a game is whether she enjoyed it or not. Like most other people, she's either enjoyed it or thought that it's a load of rubbish. She knows her football and what she's talking about.

She also knows me, and how to handle me, very well. Once,after we'd been out she asked me: "What would you like for your tea?" I decided on steak and she went home to get the tea while I went to the pub with six or seven other people for a few drinks at a place called Murphy's Bar. We stayed behind after closing time for a few more drinks and because we were enjoying ourselves playing cards, the time flew by. The next thing, she was on the phone saying tea was ready. I told her I'd be home, sat down and promptly forgot all about tea again. Another hour later she phoned up again. I said I'd be home soon and went back to playing cards. Half-an-hour later she walked in, although I didn't see her because I had my back to her. Everything went silent and she plonked down a plate in front of me said: "Here's your effing tea" and walked out to clapping and cheering. What could I do? I warmed it up in the microwave and ate it. It was lovely! They've still got the plate hanging in the pub. One of the lads even complained that she hadn't brought a sweet.

It was a laugh but it taught me a lesson. It taught me that I shouldn't take her for granted, and not just because if I don't she'll embarrass me again. At the time I thought :"What a bitch. Fancy doing that." The next day I admired here for having the face to do it. She's got guts and I respect her.

Elaine is a snob compared to me, and I don't mean that nastily, I mean that light-heartedly. When she was a kid, her family had their own house and went on holiday every year, whereas with me it was council house and no holidays. The first time I went abroad was with Liverpool on a club tour. She had the things my family always struggled for, was always comfortable.

She works very hard because she always wants the best of things. She went from a detached house to a terrace when we moved to Newport and that was a bit of a comedown for her.

I'm a very strong person and Elaine's a very strong person and we've had some arguments. I'll always remember one at Newport. I went out one night and didn't get back until 1.30 am, only to discover that she'd locked the door. I was standing there, a bit drunk, pleading with her to open the door. She just shouted something totally unladylike.

Some of the glass panels in the door had previously been smashed and I'd put up a board so no-one could get in. After about half-an-hour on the doorstep, I put my hand through the door and opened it. I went upstairs and she threw my clothes all over the place. They stayed there for a week until the peace was made and she put them back.

Wives and girlfriends have to be very tolerant with footballers. Their day off, when they could be with their other half, is often spent playing golf which is an all-day job. On the other hand, if they don't do anything and the other half doesn't work, they can be together from two o'clock until bedtime and that can be a bit monotonous.

A lot of women are attracted to footballers. Besides film and television stars and pop stars, it's probably the next best thing. Saturday afternoon is like a fashion show, with the wives and girlfriends all trying to outdo each other. You like to be someone, not a nobody, and if you can't be someone the next best thing is to be with a someone, especially for girls. And if you're a young lad and you're surrounded by girls when you go out, well, it's a bit flattering to say the least.

If you get a few new players coming to a club at about the same time, their wives tend to stick together. If just one player comes, it's very difficult for his wife, especially for the first two or three months, because she's new down here. While her husband gets to know his team-mates quite quickly because he's in every day, his wife only comes down every couple of weeks or whatever.

It's a difficult situation when the team is away and the wife has got no friends. Especially in the Westcountry, which is likely to be a long way from her family. Most wives or girlfriends tend to make friends within the club their fellow plays for or in the immediate area they live in. They are not normally in one place long enough to put down roots.

Players' wives and girlfriends cause a lot of problems within football. A lot of back-stabbing comes from players' wives. Players tell their wives certain things; players tell other players something different; and wives tell other wives the original version again. Same situation, different story. But what you find out from your wife, via the other player's wife, is the true version. My missus has always told me more about my team-mates than I have learnt from them myself.

Women tend to be a lot more open and honest than men when they chat among themselves. When wives find out that other wives' husbands are on more money it cause problems, rifts, because certain wives want to outdo certain other wives.

When Nicky Law and Steve Cherry lived at Ivybridge, their wives would never come to any do in Plymouth. Steve Cherry was not very popular in another way with players. When he was training at Nottingham Forest, some of the stories that got back to us about what he had been telling the Forest lads about Argyle were totally out of order.

When you've been in to see the gaffer, you tell other players two-thirds of the truth or half the truth about what went on. But you tell your wife the whole truth, obviously. And I guarantee that, within two weeks, the other wives will know the truth and, inevitably, their husbands will know. I've found out things about players in this way that I've had no idea about.

When a player goes in to see the gaffer, what goes on is between him and the gaffer. I might ask a player who is looking for a transfer whether anyone has come in for him, which his what he's been to see the manager about, and he'll say: "No, not really." Two weeks later it will turn out that some club has been in and offered £80,000 for him, and the player knew that although he didn't tell you. You've found out from your wife, who has found out from his wife .

That sort of grapevine can be destructive within a club, though Plymouth in the last few years is probably better than most clubs. I've known players keep their wives away from other players' wives because they don't want them to find out certain things.

One Plymouth player used to get an earbashing from his wife every day because she didn't like the situation he was in. Other players were on better money than he was. It wasn't very nice for him and it must have affected him on the park as well.

Playing away

My life is my life and if another player wants to mess around with another woman, that's up to him. If I was out with my wife and we saw another player with a bird that wasn't his wife, it's 100 per cent certain that it would not get back to his wife. With other players' wives it would get straight back.

At Newport, one of the lads was messing about with another girl while his wife was still living in another part of the country. Eventually his wife moved down, so he stopped seeing this other girl and sorted out his marriage.

About a year later, I married Elaine in Newport and all the players and their wives came to the wedding. One of the players' wives stupidly told this particular player's wife that the girl he'd been having an affair with was at the wedding. She hadn't known before that. Next thing, all hell broke loose in the toilets. It's quite funny because everyone said it was a typical Liverpool wedding - drinking all day and a fight at the end of it!

The girl who spilled the beans got a right telling off from some of the other wives. What she did was stupid. What had happened was water under the bridge. It had happened a year before and she didn't know who the girl was or even what she looked like. She didn't really even want to know. Her husband had stopped seeing her and it was all over.

John Uzzell, who is now with me at Torquay, was divorced while he was playing for Plymouth and that was a very difficult situation for some people because his first wife was very well liked by a lot of the wives. John was very open about what happened. He simply told us that he was seeing another woman.

All of a sudden, you've got to cope with his first wife not coming to the games, then him bringing his new wife. People knew his first wife and it took time to bring the new Mrs Uzzell into the circle. Women are not the "she's out, she's in" type. It's a hard thing for them. Their first reaction was probably: "There she is, she's the other woman" that sort of thing; you know what women are like.

Eventually, though, you've got to accept her, to say to yourself "okay". It takes a couple of months or so, then she's accepted and is invited to all the parties as normal. Players can accept it more than their wives can. It's quite easy for a player to come in and say: "Look. I've split up with my wife and I'm going out with someone else." That's his decision and no-one will do anything to change that.

I've been at other clubs when some players have dabbled with other players' wives and if that had ever happened at Plymouth while I was captain I would have said something because that situation is totally out of order.

Certain things happened at Plymouth while I was captain which annoyed me, involving players who are not with the club anymore.

My wife went out of her way to help another players' wife. She phoned her up and said : ``I know you're not happy here. If you want any help or want to bring your kid round here while you go out, just let us know.'' Elaine put herself out to help this person because I was captain.

She told my wife: "Thanks very much" but I got to know from another player that when she told her husband he just said "Why doesn't she just mind her own business?" I was really annoyed and pulled this guy and said she wasn't being nosey or anything, she just wanted to see if they would like any help. She was only thinking of them.

There are pressures on marriages. Every time you go out, there are girls who want to get to know you and it's very tempting. You might just intend it to be a one-night stand but if it goes on a little longer then you become involved. And when your wife finds out, the chances are the marriage will be on the rocks. That's how it happens. Nine out of ten footballers' marriages split up because of another party. There's temptations in every sphere of life but especially in football because, as I've said before, it has the appearance of being a very glamorous life.

There are women about, and I'm not having a go at women in general, who are almost soccer groupies. I can honestly say, though, that I've been faithful to my wife since we've been married. I think she believes me as well! It's something to be proud of I think.

Since we've been married, Elaine and I very rarely go out together without each other. We socialise, but we do it together. Elaine always says that if a married man is in a night-club with another couple of men, he's up to no good. Stag nights are an exception, but if you do it on a regular basis, it has the look of something a little bit naughty.

It sounds cliched, but my best friend is my wife. Honestly. We very rarely go out alone now and that's by choice. Very rarely now will you see me alone out in a pub with other people during the week, especially the players, because that's the way I want to live. Maybe I've isolated myself, I don't know. Or perhaps it all boils down to what happens on the training pitch, my competitive nature in training. I can leave behind what happens on the training ground, other people can't and that's probably why I've got few friends in the game. Funnily enough, I've always been better friends with people after they've left the club.

When Steve Cooper was at Plymouth, he was in and out of the side and kept his own counsel. Now, he stays here every time he comes down, but we were never very close when we were playing together.

Ask any professional footballer how many footballing friends they've got and they'll all give you the same answer. Footballers don't call other footballers "my friend" or "my mate". It's more of an association really. It's not 11 friends who trot out together to play every week. It's not like that. You've got to look after yourself and maybe that's where the resentment creeps in.

I'm surprised our marriage has survived in a way. We're both strong people. Elaine isn't the most unattractive woman in the world and she could get most men if she tried. She hasn't and I haven't tried to get another woman. It's a case of whether you're prepared to risk, and possibly sacrifice, everything you've got. She has even said that if she ever found out that I'd been on a one-night stand it wouldn't necessarily ruin the marriage, although it would obviously tarnish it. But I don't think I'll put it to the test.

Affairs are a different kettle of fish altogether. You look at it and ask yourself whether it is worth going out with a girl who nine times out of ten isn't better looking than your wife anyway, might wiggle her hips a little bit more, and okay, you maybe half-fancy her because you're half-drunk. Is that worth risking losing your wife, your family, your kids, your whole way of life for? At the end of the day, that's what it boils down to. I've decided it's not worth losing.

But it happens so often in football because you come into contact with so many people, so many attractive people. The people that you associate with are not the working class that come to watch the game. They are at the functions which are attended by businessmen and their secretaries, people that are willing to spend money on you because they want something from you. You go to fancy restaurants when you go out. You're mixing with people who have got money, the social classes. It is easy to go off the rails.

Master plumber

I met Elaine in a night-club at Sheffield and we've been together ever since - twelve years now. I was trying to get her to go out with one of my mates and she didn't know who I was. I kept telling her I was a plumber.

I was asking her: "Will you go out with my mate?" and she kept saying no. Then she said :"But I'll go out with you though" and that's how it started. It's funny, that. For all the girls that went out with me because I was a footballer, the girl I ended up with, and eventually married, thought I was a plumber. It was quite light-hearted and she did tell me afterwards that she knew who I was anyway, though I'm not sure.

A lot of people don't know I've been married before but I was married when I was 18. We lived with my mum and dad after the wedding and if I can give anyone a little piece of advice it would be to never do that. We lived in one room and it just didn't work out. We split up nine months later. It was a horrible situation to be in and, to be honest, probably both of us were a little bit immature to handle it. I was bringing in just £32-a-week, which wasn't enough to look after us, either.

Elaine has been good for me because she's a strong person. I might have been a little bit wayward if I had been married to anyone else, but with her I haven't.

I probably wouldn't be playing football now if it hadn't have been for her because when I was a little bit younger football didn't mean as much to me as it later did. It should have done but it didn't, about seven or eight years ago.

I remember Tom Saunders, at Liverpool, asking the young apprentices what we wanted from football. Well, what do you want when you're a young lad? Plenty of money, plenty of birds, a nice car, that sort of thing.

He used to say: "You get your football right and you'll get everything else you want." And I used to think: "Silly sod. He doesn't know what he's talking about." But he was right, exactly right.

I nearly found that out the hard way when I went through a spell at Newport when I wasn't playing. I was very frustrated and very disillusioned with football. I wasn't in the side and wasn't making a lot of money. My wife was working to keep us on a good standard of living because I wasn't doing the business.

I worked for a friend of mine in the summer, labouring, and made a living out of it. At one stage I thought:"What's playing football all about?" Thankfully things started getting better suddenly, but if it hadn't have been for Elaine standing by me through the rough period there was a chance that I might have said: "Stuff football."

Ever since, I've worked hard at playing football and scoring goals. All right, First Division football has never come my way but I've made a very good living out of the game and I'm not complaining.

I've got a nice house and great family - although we still struggle to pay the bills now and again if I don't pick up enough win bonuses.

We have a good standard of living, though. I earn *x* amount of pounds but I can double that if the team is successful, through bonuses, cup runs and promotion seasons. Footballers are on good money, a lot better than other people, but it's not loadsamoney, only enough for a very decent living. The myth about footballers being very wealthy is just that for the majority of professionals, a myth. It's a load of rubbish.

I probably wasted about two years of my career, on and off, and I might have played in the First Division if I'd listened to a few people early on. I honestly believe I'm fitter now than when I was 23.

I've achieved a lot more than a lot of other people in the game and I think that's down to my wife and family being there, for listening to me and for kicking me up the backside every now and again.

At the end of the day, you have to ask yourself: "What do you want from life? Do you want to live in a council flat and scrape a living; do you want a small house and a nice quiet life or do you want a very good standard of living for yourself and your family?"

I came to the conclusion that I wanted the best I could provide for Elaine and my kids and we've had that ever since. Like I say, even now we have to watch the pennies if we go two or three weeks without a win, though. A lot of people might not believe that but you gear yourself up to a standard of living that you're used to.

Me and mine

Thomas is too young to start playing football, although he does seem to have a natural ability with the ball. When he was two I threw him a ball, like most dads do, and he hit it straight away. It might sound daft but he seems to have inherited something!

I hope he will play football one day, although I won't push him. If he plays, I hope it will be for him and not for me. I love football and me becoming a professional footballer was the greatest thing that ever happened to my dad, but I didn't do it for him. I want Thomas to sort out his own life.

At 14, you would have thought Tammy could have achieved anything academically that she wanted. She passed three or four O-levels without studying for them and she would have got eight, even ten, if she'd studied for a few months.

At one stage it looked as though she could have gone to university, but it wasn't what she wanted. Boys, records, whatever, took over. That's the way it is. Everyone makes a choice and she made hers. You either go one way or the other.

Keeley suffers from cerebral palsy although, to look at her, you wouldn't know she's handicapped. She is never going to be able to do anything outside the family and because of that her mum is very, very protective of her.

She's 16 but has got the mentality of a child of between eight and ten and as she gets older that difference is going to continue. When she's 30, she'll have the mentality of a 15-year-old. But she is a great, great kid.

She's becoming a young woman now and she looks unbelievable when she's dressed up. That frightens Elaine because there are too many people about these days who will try to take advantage of people like her.

We've talked about going into a business, a pub or something, if and when football's finished and we've always thought Keeley will go with us and we will help her. She has been at Downham Special School, in Plymstock, where most of the others are more severely handicapped. She's helped look after the other kids and I think that has benefited her far more than any academic learning.

Jordanna and Thomas will have to go their own way when they are older. I will help them as much as I can, but I don't think it's down to mothers and fathers to make up their children's minds for them. It's down to the kids themselves.

I was brought up as a Roman Catholic in a very religious family, was baptised because my mother wanted it and went to church every Sunday until I was 16 because that's the way I was raised. I made my own decisions after I was 16.

We've had our kids baptised, not in a Roman Catholic church though, but I believe they'll make up their own minds on religion and life when they are old enough. It's no good imposing your views on them.

I would never say to my kids: "You've got to go to a Roman Catholic school. You've got to brought up as a catholic. I want you to be confirmed" all that sort of thing. The stuff I went through. I did it because my mother told me to do it and I don't think I could do that with my kids. They'll decide for themselves when they are older.

People ask what religion you are or what faith you are but I don't really know what faith is. I've got faith in myself to bring up my family knowing what's right and what's wrong but I won't follow a faith called "Roman Catholic" or "Protestant".

I'm afraid I don't believe in religion. I don't see any point in going to church when I've had my father taken away from me, my mother taken away from me and a child taken away from me.

Jordanna's a twin. Elaine had very bad toxaemia when our two girls, Jordanna and Jermaine were born and Jermaine died after nine days. It's very sad. It brings it back home to you every time you see twins.

My father smoked between 40 and 80 cigarettes a day and because of that I've never smoked a cigarette in my life, just the odd cigar after meals. My mother had a brain tumour and was very ill for a long time. She also had a stroke before the tumour was discovered which deprived her of the use of an arm and a leg.

She went into hospital and was dead within three weeks. The day my father was told he had cancer he went into hospital and he died within five days.

A turning point

After my dad died in 1983 and I'd had a couple of days off for the funeral, I was back in training and the Plymouth manager, Johnny Hore pointed out that I was looking a lot sharper than before I went away. I went back and thought about what he'd said and it dawned on me why.

My dad had never had much of a life but he devoted it all to making sure his wife was looked after and his kids were brought up properly. At his funeral, I realised how lucky I was to have escaped the rat race and to be able to give my wife and kids things that he'd never been able to give his family - all through playing football. It boiled down to me asking myself would I rather be leading the type of life he led or continuing enjoying the benefits of the life I was leading. Of course, it didn't take me long to come to the conclusion that I was enjoying a good life and getting well paid for it. Why not continue putting my utmost into it and, by doing that, get the best out of it? Looking at it that way made me determined to work hard, and it turned out better than I could have hoped. Call it a turning point if you like.

13

STIMULATING TIMES

THE FIRST time I remember seeing people take drugs before a game was very early on in my career, when I was in the reserves. Some of the older players used pills - always just before matches - although I never saw the staff give them anything.

Later, when I'd moved on, one of my team-mates was very overweight and wanted to lose weight quickly so he was given something by the club doctor, that I think were amphetamine-based tablets, to help him shed the pounds. He was given a month's prescription which I think he only took two weeks worth of.

I've seen players take pills before Football League matches, without ever knowing what they were. There was one time when a few of the lads weren't feeling too clever, and they took them about half-an-hour before the game, just to help them get through the match. The club doctor knew they were taking them, the pills were already there, at the club. But they weren't prescribed individually.

Players had the choice of taking them; no-one forced them on you.

The manger asked if we wanted them and when I asked what they were for, he told me they'd build up the heart-rate. They were known commonly as pep pills and that was it. With drug testing, it all came a little bit risky and everything stopped. I don't know if anyone takes anything now because of the random drug-testing.

Mainly, people took them to help them lose weight. Like, say, when they had been a stone overweight and they wanted to lose the excess, they would take one-a-day. Because they were only eating one meal-a-day, the drug would help them get through. Losing weight is what they were mainly used for, but one or two players did take them before matches, never at Plymouth though. The drug apparently built up your heart-rate. Players said they could always tell because they felt a little lethargic when they went out and five minutes into the warm-up or the game they could feel themselves becoming a little bit stronger than they were before.

It didn't last that long. Maybe an hour-and-a-half to two hours. All of a sudden they'd feel very tired, so they'd have a few pints after the match which would bring them back up again. I never thought it was illegal, I'm still not sure that it was. I'd known of people taking drugs and actually seen people take them, but then I was young lad and never really realised what was going on.

Like I say, team-mates took them but never on a regular basis. Always when they felt a little bit down or not quite on their best form. The second time I remember people taking anything was when there had a bit of a flu bug going round the club during the week, although everyone had got over it by the time the weekend came around.

There was no-one else in the dressing room apart from the twelve lads involved and the manager just said: "If you're feeling low, I've got something you can take. It's up to you. You don't have to take it." And he had this bottle of pills in his hand.

I don't know whether it was ethically right and it's virtually stopped since the Willie Johnston affair in the 1978 World Cup and random drug-testing. But I bet it went on, occasionally at least, at ninety per cent of Football League clubs.

When I broke my toe one summer, the gaffer told me that if I was on a diet I should take something, just to keep me going. I went to the chemists with a prescription and the dispenser asked if I knew what they were for. I just told him I wanted to lose weight. He told me not to take too many because they were very strong, and seemed pleased when I told him I was only taking one-a-day. Those were prescribed for me by a doctor, so that was all above board.

You might be called a cheat for taking something, but how do you know the other side isn't on something as well? It never entered my head that anyone was cheating, or that it was anything other than normal, because the club doctors knew about it.

There are very few footballers who use recreational drugs and if I ever found out that anyone at a club I was at was using them I'd do my best to stop it because I simply don't believe in them. You can have a drink and that should be enough. I've heard of one or two footballers who use drugs but I've never come across them personally. I go to the right sort of parties! It's one thing I've never been into or known people that have.

I've been in pubs and people have been smoking whatever it is they smoke - I recognise the smell - and I know they are relatively easily available, but I couldn't personally go out and get them now. Not the circles I'm in. For me, drugs simply aren't a turn-on, apart from alcohol. I like a drink. Drinking, gambling, fast cars, and birds all come together for footballers. One follows the other, and that's plenty of vices!

A legend in his own drinking-up time

After a match, almost without exception, you'll have a drink, and the result depends on how much you enjoy it. At home matches, where you're less likely to lose, there's always quite a reasonable atmosphere after the game. In the past at Plymouth, it was normally a case of having a few drinks and then going home because no-one tended to socialise. In the last few years it was more the case that people would have a few drinks and then find out where everyone was going for the evening.

A lot of players, especially the players with families, had a few drinks after the game and then went into town, to the Lanterns or somewhere, had a nice meal, a couple more pints and then went home. Or they had a few drinks, went home to make sure the kids were looked after, then met up later. It was a good social scene.

Here's a question. Who drinks the most, an average dockyard worker or an average professional footballer? I'll tell you the answer. A professional footballer. They can afford it and they have a lot of free time. If you haven't got a midweek game, you've got five afternoons and evenings every week to yourself. Alright, you can go swimming or shopping, but that just takes care of two afternoons. Once you've finished training at 1 pm you've got the afternoon to yourself.

At Plymouth in recent years, the players have generally got on well with each other, though that's not the case at some clubs where I've been. There's one or two who like a drink, and there's nothing wrong with that; I've always enjoyed a drink myself. But there's too much free time and too much temptation, and it's frightening to think how often you have a drink. I'm not talking about the hard stuff. It's possible to have three or four pints and sweat it off next day in training, but you can start having three or four pints a night four or five times-a-week and that's really not on.

You finish training at 1 pm and you're sat on the settee until 8 pm and you think: "What shall I do next?" Next thing, you're at the fridge getting a can, then another, just to pass time really. I've known some drinkers in my time, players who can shift ten or 15 pints-a-night. They didn't keep their fitness for too long!

Gordon Nisbet had a drink four or five times-a-week, but only two cans-a-night and he never put on an ounce in weight. He was still the quickest player at the club when he left Plymouth. I've seen another Argyle player drink 20 pints in an evening, and been amazed myself when you calculate what you've drunk on a night out. I've listened to Jimmy Greaves talking about his alcoholism and can understand what he meant by not realising how much he was getting through when he was a player, simply because he was so fit.

The only way you notice it is if you weigh yourself, because your physical appearance doesn't really change. If you then go without a drink for a couple of days, your weight goes back to normal. It's your fitness that helps you drink more, if you see what I mean. You get over it quicker because you are fitter. The amount you can drink is greater. I'm not just talking about it, I've done it.

I was drinking five or six pints-a-night, four nights-a-week when I was at Lincoln, because I was fed-up and bored. I lost a lot of fitness, I was 7 lbs overweight, and I found it easy to do. I left for Newport and Len Ashurst got hold of the situation. He pulled me in and said: "You've got a lot of ability but if you don't sort yourself out, and soon, you'll be out of the game." Len Ashurst has been one of the biggest influences on my life and I'll always be grateful to him.

It's down to the individual but footballers generally drink too much, without a doubt. Football is a very social activity, especially if you're a young lad, though how social depends on whether you're a star or an also-ran. If you're doing well and in the first-team what do you want? You want plenty of money, which you'll get for playing good football. Where do you go to meet the birds? You go to the pub, and if you go out at 7.30 pm, which young lads do, you'll probably come back at 2 am after going to a night-club. You're not talking about drinking just four or five pints in six-and-a-half hours.

It can land you in trouble but nine times out of ten the trouble has got nothing to do with footballers. People have a go at them because they are out having a drink. I've been out and had two or three pints and people have phoned up the club next day to report to the manager that I've been out getting paralytic.

At Rotherham, when we played on a Tuesday night, I was in a licensed restaurant for a meal - no drinks - a couple of days before and somebody rang up the club on Tuesday morning and said I'd been seen reeling drunk in a pub on the Sunday afternoon.

When I was at Sheffield Wednesday, Jack Charlton used to get a regular phone call every week saying I had been out at a pub. He'd ask when I was seen and it would turn out to be a Wednesday so Jack would say that's okay. If it had been a Thursday night and he'd found out it was true then he would have had a case and I'd have been done, which is right.

I've known players go out on Friday night before a match though. At Sheffield Wednesday, players used to sneak out of their hotel rooms on a Friday night to go for a drink. But if I ever hear about players doing something against club rules or going out drinking on a night when they should be laying off the booze, I will not do anything about it. I wouldn't have even when I was captain at Plymouth, not that it ever happened there to my knowledge. Players are men and are old enough to know their own minds. They know they are doing wrong if they go out. And it's up to them.

There is too much drinking. It's too easy. There's too much time on our hands, too much time with nothing else to do. And it's fair to say that we've probably got too much money. You probably wouldn't feel like drinking if you came in at 5.30 pm or 6 pm after a hard day's work. But once you are fit and you knock off at 1 pm on Wednesday, you play snooker, have three or four pints, then you go out.

I know I'm probably wrong in saying this, but I believe there's a hell of a lot of difference between drinking beer or lager and drinking spirits. We drink too much but I'd rather a player drank four pints than drank four large whiskeys. Basically, it's okay as long as you don't drink eight or ten pints every night.

When players go out together, it's invariably on a bender; you have party, a real drinking session. I know one player, a big lad, who drank 22 pints of of lager in a night. He's still alive...and still playing football!

The next day, it sweats out of you. You never weigh yourself on a Monday morning after a Saturday night out because you know you're going to be three or four pounds overweight. But, after a couple of hard sessions, you know you'll be back to your playing weight by Wednesday morning. It's not as if you're continually drinking.

I've been out with the lads and some of them have drunk nine or ten pints and that, to a lot of people, is wrong. But they don't drink at the wrong times, they drink when they can. I know other players who don't drink at all during the week but they'll have a couple of cans of lager on a Friday night, just to help them sleep. What's the difference between two lagers and two cokes on a Friday night? Drinking's alright, even before a match, if you do it in moderation.

Safety in numbers

Years ago, people used to say there were a lot of characters in the game, hard drinkers and all that. I believe there's still a lot of heavy drinkers but they are aware that if they get drunk in public, they stand a chance of getting done. You'll get hammered if you start anything in a pub. Even worse if it gets in the papers.

So you tend to go to safe houses, places where you know you'll be alright if you have one over the eight and the fellow in the pub knows you won't go over the top. It can get a bit boisterous, but because it's a safe place, you'll be alright at the end of the night. Every player's got a safe house. There's places you can go if you want to go out and have a drink, maybe get drunk, without any hassle.

Nine times out of ten, they are the local, where you can take your girlfriend or your wife, where they know who you are. You know the landlord, you'll say hello and sit in the corner and the landlord will look after you because he knows who you are. I've been in pubs with team-mates when I've been badmouthed and the landlord has told the trouble-makers to shut up, saying: "They're just in here having a drink, same as you."

I've sat down for hours with a group of lads, playing cards and drinking and the landlord has chucked people out for having a go at us. We're not causing trouble, after all, and we're spending money.

Safe houses is right. I wouldn't go down Union Street in Plymouth. I go down the Grapevine and the Prince Regent but no way would I go down Union Street on a Saturday night. I'd get slaughtered.

People know me. I walk into a place and I can feel people looking at me. I feel uncomfortable sometimes, especially if we've lost our game. You know what they are saying: "What's he doing in here drinking when they've just got beaten?"

It doesn't matter how much you drink if you are sensible and as long as you do the business on the field. Jimmy Greaves has talked about drinking a bottle of Scotch when he was playing and he was still knocking the goals in.

The more experienced professionals do lead the younger lads astray. The young lads who break into the first-team want to be involved. They look up to you in some ways and want to be doing what you're doing, like your kid looks up to you and copies what you do because he wants your respect. You can't tell the young professionals that they're out of order because you're doing it and they're over eighteen and lead their own lives. Sometimes though, they can't handle the pace and inevitably wind up legless.

When Argyle's Crazy Gang - Kenny Brown, Mark Stuart, David Byrne, Rhys Wilmot and Sean McCarthy - get going, they are the biggest kids around. I had a sponsored car which you could remove the stickers from fairly easily. If they did that once, they did it twenty times. I had to scour a multi-storey car park once before finding the stickers on top of some unsuspecting motorist's vehicle.

They were out one night and having a go at Kenny, calling him Stig of the Dump, because he's so scruffy. Kenny got up on this wall and said to Budgie (David Byrne): "Get up on this wall so we can be the same size as Rhys." Budgie just pushed him off and Kenny was left lying in this rose bush in the centre of Plymouth, unable to get up and doing nothing about it.

Another time they came out of the China Garden in Plymouth and had this mock fight, which is what they're into. Nothing serious, just horseplay. They do it at the ground as well. It's fun to watch. And their wives or girlfriends just walk away leaving them to their fighting. They're not drunk, just happy. Kenny's broken a watch before now, scrapping. Crazy Gang is about right. They're unbelievable.

They do the right thing though. They don't involve anyone else, just lark about among themselves. It might look very bad to an onlooker, but to those in the know it's just a bit of fun.

Being dealt a blow

Gambling comes from the same root as boozing. It's always been associated with footballers. For the same reason as drinking - too much time on your hands, too much money. I've always been a card player. And on three-, four- or five-hour coach trips to Argyle's away games, it was more fun than watching videos or reading a book.

At Plymouth last season we had two card schools: the heavy school and the mediocre school, the difference being the amount of money that was staked. I can remember seeing £800 pots on the table when I was with Liverpool on tour in Sweden and I knew one player who lost £1,000 in a session. The Plymouth school wasn't that sort of megabucks but you could lose £50 in a day. When you travel for four hours; play for two hours after tea because the alternative is lying on the bed watching telly; play on the way to the ground; and play for four hours on the way back, that's more than ten hours in total and the losses can mount up if you're having a bad time.

But it generally goes in cycles. We played for twelve hours on one trip and there were pots of £40 on the table but the most anyone was up at the end of that marathon was a fiver!

A lot of managers do not like gambling before a game - although the day before is alright - and I can understand their viewpoint. If you've lost £50 or £60 then he doesn't want you going on to the park thinking about the money you've lost.

I once saw a card school get out of hand. A fellow had been having a bad time but he was finally dealt a good hand and he had to borrow money to keep things going. The other fellow kept bumping the pot up and the other chap got heated saying: "You want my shirt". He was simply asked whether he was still in the game. Then he had to admit he couldn't afford it and flung the cards across the table, despite having a winning hand at last. Punches weren't thrown but the manager stepped in. He wasn't having any of more of that.

I've heard a story, which I believe to be true, about a former international player, who has been a respected Football League manager, who was caught dealing off the bottom of the pack during an overseas trip. He never played another international afterwards.

I've known a few players in my time who can spend the afternoon sitting in a betting shop. I've done that myself. When I was at Newport, I used to pick the kids up from school because Elaine was working, so I'd just sit in the bookies between the end of training and 3.30 pm.

I've always been a gambler, but never a heavy gambler. I couldn't put £50 on a horse, maybe a tenner or £20 at a push, but £50 is a bit heavy. I might do it if I'd just won £150, though.

The funny thing is, that for all its popularity among footballers, players make very poor gamblers, especially on the horses. I think gambling is part of the life-style because footballers are, by nature, very competitive people playing a competitive game. If you win, as well as it being a bit of a thrill, you can prove to someone else that you're a better tipster than they are. Horse racing is the sport of kings.

A lot of the time you will go into a betting office with other players, although I've never gambled simply because someone else does. At the end of the day, it's great if two of you walk out of a betting office with £200 each, but if you walk out with £200 and he's skint you make a big play of it. "Yeah. You beauty," you'll say, waving the notes in his face, while he'll be moaning: "I've had a nightmare". That's the competitive streak, the rivalry. You can still laugh about it as long as it doesn't get out of hand. I've never seen one lad give another £50 out of his pocket when he's had a good day and his team-mate has had a bad one, and I don't think I ever will. It's just not done. I wouldn't do it and I don't think there's many people who would accept it, if I did. That's not part of the game. They wouldn't be able to face the other lads after the story had got out, in any case.

There was one player I heard of who got into such trouble with the bookies that he had to mortgage his house to pay them off. At the other end of the scale, there's the story of Martin O'Neill, the Northern Ireland international, who took one bookie to the cleaners and the fellow had to give him his shop to pay him up. A dream or what? It was only a small bookies but Martin apparently won more than £35,000.

It's cliched, but gambling is part and parcel of being a footballer. The time and the money are both available. I would say that of the first-team squad at Plymouth last year there were only two or three that wouldn't be involved in a card school or a sweep. Martin Harvey very rarely missed a sweep when he was coach and both he and physiotherapist Malcolm Musgrove would have a pound on a horse if we'd been given a tip.

The perfect image

There are players who will not drink in public. Roger Wylde, of Sheffield Wednesday, was one who would never be seen with a pint of lager in his hand after a game. It's all about image. Managers are keen to remind you of who you are and what you represent when you're in public.

I roomed with John Matthews for three years and he'd have the odd cigarette on a Friday night. Because you're fit and in training you can overcome the effects of the odd fag. I've never seen a player smoke heavily. It's not good for you and it presents the wrong image. Image is important to kids: it's important to other people. Think about it. The pub manager never has a pint in his hand, only a half. Image. You don't just represent yourself when you attend a function - you represent your club, so you're clean shaven and you wear a tie. Image.

I had a letter from a 65-year-old lady who had seen me on television, saying how much she'd enjoyed the interview and how nice it was to see me looking smart and presentable. People do notice. It portrays a good image, not just for yourself but for your club as well.

A lot of players hate wearing ties, and the first thing they do when they're out of the public eye is to yank the tie off. Five days a week they wear a tracksuit and everything is very casual, very loose. Saturday is different. They wear a suit or a jacket and tie. Like a businessman in reverse. Ken Brown introduced a rule that we didn't wear jeans to Argyle training sessions. Even in private, there is an image to be maintained.

When you travel away and 11 players walk into a hotel wearing identical club tracksuits, people know you are a football team and you are all together. It's an image. It looks horrible if you arrive at a Post House hotel on a Friday night all wearing different coloured tracksuits. You have to portray an image to people and it is the image of a disciplined, professional outfit.

Beards are hated in football. I don't know why, but the current trend is not to like a fellow running round with a face full of hair. It doesn't look right. Moustaches are okay but not beards. I find it difficult to think of any player in the entire league who has got a beard. Ken Brown even expected us to be clean shaven on match day as well. Image again.

The day after Ken Brown introduced the no jeans rule, Andy Thomas arrived at the ground for training wearing a pair of denims. It wasn't two fingers up to the staff, he'd just forgotten and was fined for it. I did know one player once who used to come in every day flouting one rule or another and he was fined £2-a-day, just for the pathetic sake of having a go at the establishment.

As a manager, you have to have certain rules and regulations, just like you do in other businesses. They might sound trivial but things are not going the way you want them to if you don't enforce the little rules. You, as manager, have to portray an image with the resources you've got. The best way of doing that is to have a rulebook which lets everyone know what they can and can't do. I would certainly have a rulebook if I was a manager. It probably stops individuality because you are grown men, not kids. But really you, as an individual, are not more important than the club as a whole anyway.

The rulebook, which Ken Brown introduced, has remained in force since David Kemp took over. The new boss wasn't that harsh over bookings and sendings-off because he was so busy with the rest of his job. He had a lot on his plate. But the rules are Plymouth Argyle club rules, not Ken Brown's rules, even though the rulebook is signed by the previous manager.

I think Plymouth is one of the few clubs that hasn't got a club blazer and greys, which is a shame. I think nothing looks smarter than players arriving at a ground or coming out after a match with the same gear on and I think it would go down well at Plymouth.

The staff are all governed by the same rules as the players so it's not a case of do as I say, but do as I do, which is fair. They abide by the rules that they have set.

When I was captain, I used to get crucified because I had to collect the fines levied on breaches of rules and regulations. There are certain things you can do and certain things you must not do. One of Ken Brown's pet hates was people taking off their boots without untieing their laces. You couldn't walk into the shower without flip-flops, either. That was a rule introduced because of hygiene. Plymouth players can't wear club gear except at club functions, so if one player sees another walking out with a club tracksuit on, he'll get fined.

At Argyle, you're meant to fold up your kit. There's a £2 fine if it's all over the floor. Walking from the dressing room to the training pitch with your boots on is also a fineable offence, and there's sense behind that because we normally have aluminium studs which can quickly become sharp and dangerous after walking on concrete.

Being late will cost you £5 and being 15 minutes late will relieve you of a tenner, but most of the fines are £1 or £2 and at the end of the day all the money goes into a players' pool anyway. Nearer the Christmas do which the fines finance, the players tend to throw anything in. If you fart you get fined a quid.

They're only little fines but, I tell you what, you ought to hear the arguments that there are over a few quid. Mark Stuart was late once because Kenny Brown, who normally picked him up on the way to training, was off with tonsillitis. Mark said Kenny should pay the fine for not picking him up and it took the gaffer to explain to him that Kenny wasn't late, Mark was, the fine would come out of his wages if he didn't pay it.

Generally though, it's a good thing. Everyone gets involved. If you try walking to the showers without your flip-flops you can bet that someone will see you and report you to the fines' committee. It gets players together and it achieves certain objectives. By introducing the rule about folding your kit away, Ken Brown got a tidier dressing room, which is what he wanted. He used to say: "You wouldn't do it in your own home would you?" although I think some of the wives might not agree!

We couldn't play with a football in the dressing room and that might sound a bit daft but there was a reason for that as well. If you start belting the ball round the room and you break a light bulb, there's glass lying around and you could find yourself getting cut badly.

There's a lot of good banter and everyone's involved but, if anyone on the fines committee gets done, their fine is doubled. Team spirit. It's your own fault if you don't fit in a dressing room, it means you don't want to fit in. You can't blame anyone else if it happens. It's down to the individual concerned.

Tommy Argyle

At Plymouth recently, there wasn't anyone who didn't fit in. Everyone got on, and enjoyed going out for drinks, with each other and you can't tell me that was not good for the atmosphere in the dressing room.

There was no-one who just sat in the corner of the dressing room and didn't get involved. Adrian Burrows might have come into that category when he first came from Northampton Town. He was shy, very introverted and he could have stayed that way forever, But he didn't. Now he's a right bastard like the rest of them! In fact, he's the biggest micky-taker in the world.

The reason they call Adrian "Shades" is because he'd always turn up in these bloody terrible sun-glasses when he first came to the club. Or he'd come down the pub with a hat on, or yellow trousers or some other wonderful garb. A right weirdo. We all thought he was gay, because he was very quiet and wasn't married, didn't even have a girlfriend. But he proved everybody wrong.

Little Leigh Cooper, the mums' and dads' favourite,is known as the Gibbon because of his hairy armpits. And Kevin Summerfield's nickname is the Skeleton. If there's a broom in the corner of the room you can bet your mortgage someone'll turn round and say: "Shut up Summers."

Kevin Hodges is the Dog, don't ask me why.

I've got about fourteen nicknames. It used to be the rent boy, because I collected the fines when I was captain. Then there was the stage when one or two of the lads would arrive in the dressing room wearing capes after I'd been made captain and scored a couple of goals. The newspaper headline read "Captain Marvel."

The Old Man is another one, naturally, and Kenny Brown called me Tommy Argyle. Some of the lads cut out a picture that appeared in the programme of a fan escorting an old lady out of her house and stuck it on the noticeboard with the caption: "Come on Tom, just one more game" underneath. After we'd pulled Arsenal out of the hat in the Littlewood's Cup, one of the lads sent a letter to John Brimacombe. He opened it up and all it contained was a picture of David Rocastle!

Winning team: Dave Smith and I salute Argyle's return to the Second Division in 1986. Now we want promotion together at Torquay United

A night to remember: The happy Argyle dressing room after beating Bristol City 4-0 to win promotion.

Bubbling over: Russell Coughlin and I drink to Argyle's promotion success.

TT phones home: Ringing my wife from a hotel room on an away trip.

The first team: At home with Elaine, Thomas, Tammy, Keeley and Jordanna.

Giving something back: With the staff and pupils of Stuart Road Primary School.

Captain's mate: Posing for a typical press photograph with the captain of HMS Invincible, Mike Gretton.

Leading from the front: Preparing to do battle with Swindon Town.

14

RACISM AND HOOLIGANISM

I DON'T understand racism in football. Sometimes I find that coloured players who say they have been called a black bastard don't tell you what they have said to the other player. I've actually said that to a player and had them come back at me. I've called a player a black bastard - as an insult, not out of hatred - and they've come back with: "Yeah, your wife loves one, doesn't she?" I've also had a coloured centre-half call me white trash. It's intimidation, not racism, and it goes on in football. I'm not a racist.

Paul Chambers was out of digs when I came down to Argyle and he came and stayed with Elaine and me. I wouldn't have allowed him in the house if I was racist. I think people talk too much about racism in football. I don't care whether a player's white, black or green; if he's a good footballer, he's a good footballer.

I've said things to white centre-halves to get them going. "You'd better watch yourself or you'll get an elbow in the face", that sort of thing. That is intimidation. People have said to me: "Come near me and I'll break your leg" as I've walked onto the park. That happens in football and if anyone tries to tell me otherwise, I'll call him a liar because it goes on and it has been going on for years. It proves whether you're a man or not because if you listen to it and believe it you won't be in the game for as long as I have. You'll fold.

I'm not bothered about colour, especially in sport. In boxing, cricket, football, athletics, whatever, if he's the best man, he's the best man, and that's it. Calling someone a black bastard is a way of getting at someone. You call a someone a fat bastard because he's overweight, you call someone a black bastard because he's black. It's not overt racism. It's an insult and an easy way of insulting someone.

There's been a lot of coloured lads at Plymouth and there's never been any animosity directed towards them from the players. I think that's general within the game. Calvin Plummer came to Plymouth from Nottingham Forest and someone said something derogatory to him in a joking sort of way and he turned round and said: " Whatever you say to me, I've heard it all before, so don't bother." and that was it.

There is racism on the terraces and it is unfortunate. It's still a minority who indulge, though. We played Stoke once and they had two coloured lads called Carl Saunders and Tony Ford playing for them. The Plymouth fans jeered them and threw bananas and everything. All the time Calvin was standing on our right wing. They don't realise, they are too stupid to realise, that when they were having a go at the opposition's black players, they were having a go at Calvin too. It's the same in reverse when we play away. I've noticed it especially at Stoke and Leeds.

I don't really think about racism on the terraces because it doesn't really affect me, and I know it didn't affect Calvin either because he'd heard so much of it.

It never crosses my mind about people chanting on the terraces. They pick on a player's colour because he's black: people have a go at me because I score goals regularly and they don't want me to. So they have a go at me because they think they are going to upset me. That's why they do it. Nowadays, it's easier because there are more coloured players playing.

I always remember Gordon West playing for Everton at Liverpool, where the home fans called him a big fat woman. They used to throw handbags at him every time he played at Anfield, and the Everton fans used to throw bananas when Ian St John played at Goodison because they reckoned he looked like a little chimp. So throwing bananas is not new, just more noticeable because there's more black players about. More targets.

Mixing politics and sport

Politicians create more problems in sport than they help solve. What is happening in South Africa is awful, apartheid is terrible, but you can't tell me that it is not right to get sportsman out there to teach kids sport and give a lot of people, whether they're black or white, some pleasure.

I don't agree with politics in sport. It's intertwined, I know, but it shouldn't be. Two people or eleven people playing against each other on equal terms, whether they are black white or sky-blue pink, is the essence of sport.

I've never been in a situation where I've had to ask myself whether I'd play football in South Africa for money. I can't say whether it's right or wrong, but I can't see why I shouldn't do it if it just boils down to giving a lot of people some pleasure. Kevin Keegan gave two fingers to the system when he went over there and coached 20,000 black kids and I don't see why other people shouldn't follow his example. Kevin Keegan didn't need the money, I know that.

I had a lot of time for Kevin Keegan. There were a lot of stories that went around about him, saying how nasty he was, but I knew the fellow and he was one of the nicest people you could wish to meet. When I was at Liverpool, he was doing an article for the Observer newspaper on soccer skills and he roped me and a couple of other youngsters, Brian Kettle and Tony Maguire, in to do some photographs which were to be used as illustrations. It took an afternoon and he gave the four of us a week's wages for helping him. I've heard the stories about him welshing on bets, but I don't believe them for a minute because he's a hell of a nice fellow and even now there's not many people in Liverpool who will have a go at him. What he did for three apprentices was typical of the guy.

Fighting talk

People who go to football for fights are not football fans. It's as simple as that. What annoys me is that everyone else who goes to stand on the terraces gets branded along with the small minority of idiots who cause trouble.

The idiots go to the ground after a couple of pints beforehand and they are not interested in the game. They go just to start fights and because of a handful of idiots do that, the majority of people get tarred with the same brush.

It's not just football either. It's everywhere you go. Even abroad. I remember seeing a television report where a lad abroad had stabbed a waiter. The report said the lads they were looking for in relation to the incident were wearing football jerseys and the inference was that they were football fans. Anyone can wear a football shirt, it doesn't mean they are football supporters.

I've spoken to kids who've told me they go to games just for a fight. They are not supporters; they are just idiots. We went through a phase were the media publicised it too much. I know it is news, but the more it was in the papers, the more they wanted to do it.

Now, there's probably less violence connected with football than there has ever been. I can't remember the last time I've seen someone turfed out of a ground for fighting, especially at Plymouth. You used to see it all the time. There's more fighting outside grounds than there is inside these days, but that's nothing new either.

When I was an apprentice at Liverpool, you could guarantee that every time Liverpool and Everton played each other Stanley Park, which is between the two grounds, would be full of fans from Liverpool and Everton beating the brains out of each other. This was years and years ago, and it was never publicised. I'm talking about what I know and what I've seen. Isolated fights outside the ground were stopped, but there were one or two hundred people fighting in Stanley Park. It was regarded as normal.

I've seen up to fifty kids roaming the streets of Liverpool as skinheads but then they were referred to as bovver boys, not football hooligans. Now, all of a sudden when trouble breaks out and people are wearing football shirts, they are automatically football hooligans, whether it's in the proximity of a match or not. It annoys me because there are far and away more good people involved in football than bad, and the majority are penalised because of the tiny minority of idiots.

I was brought up in an area that was based on hooliganism. I wasn't a fighter at school because I was more interested in playing sports, but I know friends of mine who would leave school, take off their shoes, put on bovver boots and go and fight another school, still in school uniform. That was the area I grew up in. These people all grew up together.

You didn't walk into some of the pubs I used to go into in Liverpool, you weighed in! When I was going out with my first wife, we visited a pub called the Boundary, at the top of the place where I was brought up. Grant Road, in the Dovecote area of Liverpool. I was only 17 and I was stood at the bar buying a drink when this fellow came up with what I thought was a iron bar. That was bad enough but when I turned round he was pointing this thing at someone. It was a shotgun. I pulled my wife out of the pub straight away and as we left we heard this thing go off and a window shattering. That was my local pub!

That sort of thing happened all over the place. I was brought up with this and so were all my friends. I was lucky, I never really had a problem because I was a professional footballer and I played for Liverpool. If I had a reserve game, I'd go home and change and go down to the local for a couple before going into town. No-one used to say anything to me. I'd never have any bother because I was playing for Liverpool. Some of the lads I was talking to were involved in fighting. They were working hard for very little money and I don't know whether they resented it, but fighting was their way of getting rid of some pent-up aggression. But nothing happened to me because football bridged the divide.

I don't like hooliganism. The people who cause trouble are not fans of a club or even fans of football. They use football as an excuse to fight. The people who have talked to me about the trouble they cause are normal people in normal jobs and all they can talk about is violence, having a fight. They tell me they like football but can't wait for the fights afterwards. No-one should go to football to have a fight.

It's got nothing to do with the actual game and it brings the whole profession into a bad light. You can't combat it totally. Why can't they go and watch a game, have a few pints afterwards and go home? A lot of the time they attack people who are genuine supporters. The people that cause trouble at football matches are mindless idiots, nothing more, nothing less.

Europe reckons England is responsible for all the hooliganism problem but that is rubbish. It's always been there, in every country. Go to Holland and you'll find that the hooligans there are far, far worse than the hooligans in this country. Yet it's always the English that get blamed. The English disease.

Maybe footballers are at fault, maybe they could do more to clear it all up, though I don't know how. Politicians should make the penalties more severe, but banning people from grounds won't work because they'll simply cause aggro outside the ground if they are intent on violence.

Police and clubs are a lot more organised in getting people into grounds and away from them after the match these days. I feel sorry for the little people who just come in threes and fours and are jumped on by other people who are not supporters but who want a fight.

Under whose influence?

I've been scared on the pitch once or twice. The worst time was at Newport. We were playing Swindon in the final game of the season and Swindon had to win to stay in the Third Division. Then the referee gave a penalty which I had to take in front of the Swindon fans, who were pretty angry.

As I was preparing to take the penalty, they began knocking the advertising billboards down, obviously intent on swarming onto the pitch and, I don't know, trying to get the game stopped or something. About 20 or 30 cops came across to stop them actually reaching the pitch. I thought they were after me because I was taking the penalty, and that was quite a scary thought.

I took the penalty and they went down. The newspaper headlines the next day read: "Tynan puts Swindon down" although I wouldn't say it was entirely my fault they were relegated. Maybe they would have done better if they'd won a few more games during the season! (I met a bloke on holiday three years later and he asked me what I did. When I told him I was a professional footballer he said: "Oh yeah, I remember you. You're the bloke who put us down.")

I honestly think that if some of the fans could have got on the pitch and pinched the ball or had a go at me, they would have done. What would you think if 50 people were trying to run at you? The police moved that quickly they managed to get it in hand, I took the penalty and that was that.

People went through a phase when they looked for something to blame for all the problems. They blamed players' behaviour, but I believe that a bad refereeing decision can cause more trouble on the terraces than anything a player is capable of doing.

Do players have an obligation to try and prevent trouble? If you look at it coldly and think about it, you come to the conclusion that you do have a responsibility not to let anything happen on the park that might lead the fans to misbehave. But it's difficult because you don't have too much time to think during the heat of battle. You react. If you're kicked, your reaction is to kick back. I'm not talking about off-the-ball incidents but if someone goes in hard on you than you've got to do exactly the same thing back. If you don't, the fans will be the first to tell you that you're letting the side down.

It's difficult to remember you've got an obligation to the fans during a nasty match. You have got responsibility but you have got to give as good as you get because it's a professional game and you are after a result which, at the end of the day, is the yardstick by which the fans will judge you. I think they understand what goes on.

I was glad to see the membership scheme take a fall. I couldn't find one player who was in agreement with it and a lot of managers were against it as well. Maybe there should be some membership scheme where a fan is a member of the club he or she supports so that you can show it to a copper if he asks you where you're from. But a membership card to get through turnstiles was never going to be practicable. It would have been slow, unpredictable and far from foolproof. Even at Plymouth, there would have been queues and queues and queues of people outside, wanting to get in as soon as possible, and that would have been nothing compared to what would have been the case at Liverpool, or Manchester or London with four or five times the number of people.

15

PROFESSIONALISM

SOMETIMES YOU can go through a game, work very hard and come off feeling physically and mentally very tired. You can go play in other games when you haven't had to work very hard but you've had a lot of physical contact and that makes you feel very tired as well. Or you can go through a game and have an absolute nightmare and that, surprisingly, also makes you feel tired, mentally more than anything else. Generally, football is very tiring although just how tired you feel afterwards depends on what sort of game you've had, how much you're involved and how much you do off the ball.

I'm on a high when I come off the field after a game. I've played 90 minutes of football, I've worked hard and I come off sweating and for at least two or three hours afterwards I'm on an upper. One way of bringing myself down is to have two or three pints.

You always feel stiff an hour after the game but you never come in and slump down in a corner totally knackered. It's hard to know whether you've actually given everything that you've got because you always feel you could play more. The Plymouth lads were absolutely shattered when Arsenal beat us 6-1 in the Littlewood's Cup last year but, I tell you what, we wouldn't have felt like that at all if we'd won. That was pure mental tiredness.

If needs be, you can find extra resources. The ones that can't are the ones that are going to be on the losing end. People say you should put the same effort in no matter what the state of the game and you do try running around, putting your tackles in, working hard. But goals can knock you down and goals can lift you up. I'm knackered when I come off at the end of a game but if I had to do an extra half-hour I could do it.

You don't come off a pitch aching all over, although you probably do ache when you go to bed at midnight. A lot of the tiredness is in the mind because your body is physically fit anyway. In games themselves you get a lot of rest spaces, at stoppages and throw-ins for instance. In some games when you are two or three up and you're coasting, you don't actually work as hard as you did in the first ten minutes because you know you don't need to.

And it goes without saying that all players don't work equally hard. Some work consistently much harder than others. Someone like Mark Stuart, for instance, doesn't do a lot of work when he hasn't actually got the ball, so he might not feel as tired at the end of a game as I do. I have to do a lot of running. Age comes into it too. The younger you are, the easier it is.

Whether you're a good player or a bad player, a manager will always say that if you give 100 per cent then no-one will knock you for effort. Lack of effort comes into two categories. Some players won't run back and get their tackles in but they'll run when they're on the ball and they'll make runs off the ball, so it's not always easy for the supporters to tell he's not giving everything. The other lack of effort is basically pure laziness. Some players just stroll about showing a total lack of interest in the game and won't do anything unless they are given the ball.

I don't believe eleven players ever go out on to a football pitch believing there's nothing to play for, however meaningless the game is. There's no question of just going out to enjoy the match or go through the motions. Managers will know that and so will the fans. They're not daft. They will see through that. You never go out with a collective attitude anyway. I suppose individually it might be in the back of your own mind that there's nothing to worry about because you there's nothing hinging on a particular match. But it shouldn't. You're a professional footballer and you're doing a professional job.

I'm not always professional in some of the things I do. Drinking for one. And I'm a bit of a hothead and I do things in training which I shouldn't do. I've kicked one or two players, my own team-mates. Not often, probably once or twice a week on average. It's totally unprofessional but my temper has got the better of me. That's the way I am. Sometimes, I can go right over the top.

I had a good start when I moved to Rotherham. It was another good little club and within three months I'd scored 17 goals. Things came to a head after an incident in training between myself and a defender called Phil Crosby. The press had got wind that something had happened but the manager, Norman Hunter was telling reporters nothing except that it was a matter between him and a player. I made statement - maybe I shouldn't have done without his permission - that myself and Phil Crosby had had a fight, that I'd butted him and he'd needed stitches to his eye, but that there was no rift between me and the manager.

Norman Hunter had me in his office straight after the original incident and said:"Right, these things happen in training. It doesn't matter." He didn't even fine me. He pulled me in the day after the press had got wind of it, told me he didn't want me training with the first team and that I was on the transfer list.

But all he told the press was that the matter was between me and him and was an internal thing, instead of going public. People jumped to the conclusion that there had been trouble between me and the manager, personally, which there hadn't.

Responding to orders

I'm a sportsman. I'm getting paid for what I do, what I like doing, but it's a professional sport and you've got to act professionally. Our rulebook is the professional standards which the manager believes are our professional guidelines and which should be adhered to.

In every way, shape and form, you are asked to be a professional. Ken

Brown ordered us not to walk round Plymouth with ripped jeans and horrible tee-shirts. You have to dress respectably if you are known and likely to be recognised. Anything a manager asks a player to do within football is called professionalism. I've been in a dressing room when the manager has asked one of my team-mates to clog one of the opposition players. That is professional. They would do it to you if you don't do it to them first, that's that. One of the worst things to happen to the game was when they started handing out stiff penalties for the professional foul.

If an opposition player went through one -on-one with just the goalkeeper to beat outside the box and I was a manager, I would expect my player to bring him down. I've been told to do it myself and I would have let the manager down if I hadn't carried out his instructions when the situation arose. It's the way it is. I've had a go at a team-mate because he's let a player go through in that situation. If a player goes past me and he's only got the goalkeeper to beat, I will bring him down because that is the way I am. Anyone should do that, I don't care what you say.

People like Jimmy Hill make me sick. He's been in the game so long, been through it all himself as a player and a manager, and he knows exactly what it's like. He's been through the mill himself and knows what the professional game is all about. Now he's on telly trying to clean up the game.

It's been going on for such a long time and people annoy me when the say it should be stopped now. If Jimmy Hill was a manager and a fellow went through one-on-one with the goalkeeper to beat I wonder if he would expect his centre-half to be a gentleman and let him go through. I say he wouldn't.

I don't like it when someone goes clear from halfway after a decent move and someone has bodychecked him to break the move down. There is a slight difference between that and what I'm talking about, though maybe not a lot. From the halfway line, the defender has still got time to get back.

When Plymouth played Brighton last season, Kevin Bremner went through because Adrian Burrows let him past. Ten thousand supporters were asking themselves: "Why didn't he bring him down?" They expect it. There's no such thing as being too professional. Is it professional to let a player go through when you could foul him? I say it isn't.

Willie Young, the Arsenal defender, did the right thing when he brought down West Ham's Paul Allen in the 1980 FA Cup Final. If I was Paul Allen I'd turn round and say: "What an effing pillock you are." If I was an Arsenal player I would have said: "Well done." That's me. If someone goes through and scores, everyone in your own team and all your fans will ask why you didn't foul him to stop him. Believe anything else and you're talking about players being gentlemen and it's not a gentlemen's game. It's dog-eat-dog, man against man and you'll do your utmost to stop another man, even if it's outside the rules.

Shirt-pulling and ankle-tapping go on every week, every game you play in. It's acceptable. It's as much part of the game as free-kicks and throw-ins and players accept it, there's no getting away from that. Managers teach players things which are outside the rules, like holding off people with your arms. You can get away with it every time if it's done properly. It boils down to being a professional. The more you win, the more you earn. If you can win more by bending the rules to your advantage, so be it. The average punter doesn't see everything that goes on. He doesn't see, for instance, the opposition defender whack me in the back every time a ball's played up to me. I guarantee that I'll get knocked illegally in the back between ten or twenty times during a game. The defender will also get away with jumping on you because he's running into the ball and the referee will let it go.

Jack Charlton taught me something that was illegal and it worked for me about three times. You put your hand on the post when you're lining up for a corner and then use the post to lever you up when you jump. Jack said he used to do it all the time and I've done it a few times since he told me about it. It's an unfair advantage because you are using the post to attack the ball. The referee doesn't see it because you let go of the post as you lever yourself up.

I'm talking about little things. I wouldn't punch a player or stamp on him if I could without the referee seeing. The more serious incidents like punching people and use of the elbow are disappearing from the game, thank goodness. That's breaking the rules, not just bending them.

Staying on and sendings-off

There's no secret to avoiding injuries, although I do believe you mustn't allow yourself to become intimidated because you'll get kicked out of the game if you do.

Funnily enough, I think football has got less physical as it has progressed. In the 60s and 70s, when the likes of Martin Harvey were playing, people got kicked left, right and centre.

The Football League has combated the tackle from behind - years ago I used to come in after a match with bruises all down the back of legs - and so I very rarely take a bad tackle nowadays because I've got my back to the goal most of the time.

That's one reason why I don't get injured. Another is that I never keep hold of the ball long enough for anyone to kick me. That's the way I've been brought up, right from my Liverpool days. The way I've been taught is to control the ball, get rid of it as soon as you can to a shirt, and get in the box. And that's what I've always tried to do.

I've only ever been elbowed twice in my career, which hasn't really resulted in anything, and I've only had two injuries in my life, once in America and once in my first spell with Plymouth, and both of those were twists which injured my ligaments.

I do know how to look after myself though - you've got to - but it's just instinct, something that comes with experience.

I think defenders respect me. Certain centre-backs will let you do what you want as long as it's in front of them. Others will get so close to you it's untrue. It depends on what their managers have told them or the way they have learnt to play. But at the end of the day, if you score goals they've got to respect you.

People take age into account too much. It doesn't matter how old you are as long as you are doing the business. It annoys me that people think you're supposed to pack up just because you're 34 or 35. It's a load of rubbish. I'll play for as long as I can. Norman Hunter, Dave Smith and Len Ashurst have all told me: "When you get older, stay clear of injuries, keep yourself fit and you can play for as long as you want."

I've been sent off once or twice for a couple of things. I got my marching orders while I was at Argyle for spitting at a Lincoln player. I thought long and hard about how stupid I was and nothing like that has happened since. I was sent off against Bradford for a second bookable offence and I think it was a bit harsh. Dave Smith didn't even fine me afterwards because he asked a lot of people about the incident and none of them thought I deserved to be sent off. He also studied the referee's report before making his mind up. It was the first bad tackle in the game.

The referee didn't know anything about the spitting incident until one of my own team-mates told him about it. One of the Lincoln players said that I had spat at this player and one of the Plymouth players said to the ref: "Yes, that's right, he did." What happened was the lad knocked me in the back and I turned round while I was on the floor and spat at him. The referee couldn't have seen a thing because he was following the ball.

My team-mate Lindsay Smith told me afterwards it was one of my team-mates who'd confirmed to the referee what had happened although he couldn't be sure exactly who it was. There was lot of animosity in the team at the time and I've narrowed it down to one of three people, only one of who is still playing these days. Anyway, it cost us two points because we were 2-0 up when it happened and we drew the match 2-2.

Double standards

There are two sets of rules that operate in a game of football. Those that exist in black and white and those that are accepted by the players and, sometimes, the referees.

It looks clean when two players run for a ball, but it's not because the centre-half and you are both using your arms to gain an advantage. Coaches even coach you to use your arms to hold off opponents and that, strictly speaking, is illegal. You get away with it because you are not actually pushing, just holding someone off. A centre-half will come through you when he goes for the ball because he's been told to, it's been taught to him. It's part of the game and there's no point getting upset about it.

Appealing to the referee is also part of the game. Everyone should appeal for everything, whether they think they are going to get the decision or not. Sometimes it goes for you because referees are not perfect and they make mistakes like the rest of us. They are under pressure. They're going to have to make to make a decision one way or another when two opposing sets of players are shouting for their ruling. Sometimes you know you the ball has gone out of play off your own player but you shout: "Our ball, ref" because it forces him to make a decision. It's fair because both teams do it. You're not conning him. You're asking for decision and sometimes it goes for you, sometimes it doesn't. If you go into a 50/50 tackle and the ball spins away, the first thing you will do is claim the throw-in, and so will your opponent. It's a 50/50 decision that the referee has got to make.

Sometimes even in yourself you might think, or even know, that it isn't your ball - you know you're the last one to touch the ball - but you'll win the decision from the referee. It's not conning the referee. I'll ask the referee for a decision if I think there's a possibility that it might go my way rather than if I simply think it's my decision.

If I go through on the goalkeeper in the penalty area and the defender tackles me, I'll claim a penalty whether I think it's a penalty or not. So many times you've seen a penalty given and you think the decision is a bit harsh, or you've seen something happen in the box that is a definite penalty but the referee hasn't given it. Sometimes it goes for you and sometimes it goes against you. I'll always claim if I think I can get a decision.

If I'm in the penalty area and I know I've been tackled cleanly but I think I can get a penalty if I take a dive, I'll do it. It's never as clear cut as it seems. If I go through and I've touched the ball and I'm tackled, I'll ask for a penalty. If someone tackles you totally cleanly, you can't do that because you just look a fool. It's not a gentlemanly game and there's no point in splitting hairs about what's right and wrong. If a player catches me with his leg and I go down and get a penalty and I know it wasn't a penalty I'm not going to say: "It wasn't a penalty ref."

I'll give you an example of where you can con the referee if you're clever enough. Sometimes you can get away with it and sometimes it looks so blatant it's laughable. The ball comes into your feet; you half ride the tackle then all of a sudden you fall down. That is conning the referee because you've looked for the leg to fall over. I don't do it myself because I'm not very good at it, but some players are.

I know a lot of people say I get a lot of decisions because I go down when a player tackles and often win a free-kick, but I don't know whether that is the case.

It's easier to con the referee in the opposition's final third of the field than anywhere else. Many decisions, especially when it comes to tackles, are hardly ever clear cut. You've got the ball, the defender's leg has come across you and the ball and you fall over. You make the most of it. That's not conning the referee. If someone tackles you totally cleanly, then you're left standing anyway. But if the defender goes through you and takes the ball and the man, you're on the floor and a decision is required.

Getting away with it

When my former Argyle team-mates Leigh Cooper and Kevin Summerfield broke their legs, the referees concerned said they were challenged fairly but I can't go along with that. In my opinion, both tackles were over the top and totally out of order. There are some things in football that referees just don't understand.

Barry Horne was genuinely sorry for the tackle which broke Leigh's leg in the match against Portsmouth. I've seen the letter he sent and it was very moving, personally written from one professional to another. I thought Graeme Sharp's behaviour was was totally out of order. Kevin Summerfield was stretchered off in agony after Sharp tackled him, but Sharp never asked how he was after the game.

There are some things that players get away with, that referees never see because they're never close enough to the ball to see them. The two linesmen never see things either. Players know the difference between intent and a fair challenge and they know there are certain players who go over the top. That is totally unacceptable to a majority of professionals.

There are rules within rules, players' rules within the official rules. A game wouldn't flow at all if the referee picked up on everything illegal that happened in a match. It would be all stop-start. Referees see things and let them go for the sake of a flowing game, but it could be argued that in doing that they run the risk of losing control.

In one Argyle game last season, Sean McCarthy played a one-two with Kenny Brown and the lad took his legs. The referee waved play on but he came back and pulled the lad after the passage of play was completed, told him he'd seen what had happened and not to do it again. To me, that was a great piece of refereeing. He had achieved the aim of letting the game flow but also spoken to the offender. He saw it, let it go, waited, and then pulled the lad. He did everything right, but very few referees will do that. It doesn't happen very often.

A centre-half can come through you and clatter you to the ground with a really bad foul. But if you get up and score then he won't book the lad even if he deserves a booking. It's a case of the end result cancelling out the bad tackle.

Referees are trying hard to be professional and enhance the game but every referee interprets the rules in a different way, their own way, which can make life very hard for you. Certain referees foul you for certain things. I do a lot of backing in to defenders and I can get away with it the whole match long with some referees. Other referees penalise me every time.

There's a move which certain teams do. The ball is deliberately kicked into touch so the trainer can get on to treat an injured team-mate. When play re-starts, the opposition throw the ball to the team that has put it into touch. The continentals have been doing it for years, even in big World Cup games. We did it more than a few times ourselves last season.

I think it should go on, but Martin Harvey, who has been in the game a long time, takes the opposite view. Give it back to them when they've knocked it out? Who are they kidding?

I would be all for it for it to become an actual rule that, if someone's injured and the ball is put deliberately out of play, it should be given back, or for it to be agreed between the managers beforehand. It's sportsmanship, and football can still be a surprisingly sporting game. You can go through a game when there's not even one bad tackle; you shake hands at the end and it's been great, a joy to play in.

People can make small gestures of sportsmanship. One thing which I sometimes do is to bring the ball back for the free-kick when I've been given offside. I tell you what, it is really appreciated, judging from the crowd's reaction,

Another sporting gesture is to pick the other fellow up after you've fouled him. Coaches teach you that. They tell you that if you clatter someone to the ground, pick him up and shake his hand. The cynical people will say that you area only doing it to avoid getting into trouble with the referee. Only you will know whether you mean it.

I've been irresponsible at times. I've been in teams that have been absolutely battered and the centre-half's given me a rough time all afternoon and I've been so frustrated that I've walked off at the end without shaking hands. It happens.

I'll never ever shake hands with Mark Aizlewood again. When he was captain of Leeds United and I was the Argyle captain, he refused to shake hands because of remarks attributed to me in the Leeds press which were about a year out of date anyway. All I'd said was that I didn't think Leeds were good enough to go up. And I was talking about the previous season.

If you win a match, you go towards your own players, naturally, and clap the crowd to show your appreciation to them. You then shake hands with the opposition players, if they're still on the pitch, as you go in to the dressing room. You just want to get off the pitch as soon as possible if you've been beaten 2-0 and you've had a bad game and you might forget your manners, but it's frustration, not bad sportsmanship because you've lost.

Tommy Smith was a character at Liverpool, a serious man and a hard footballer but someone who was invariably laughing and joking. He enjoyed his football. Dave Gwyther, at Newport, was another character. As dour as hell he was. But everything is too serious now, even at our level, and money is the main reason.

We still have a laugh and a joke off the field but on the field it's all changed. You used to be able to have a laugh with referees but you can't any more. Some of the referees are so serious that if you jump all over a fellow and jokingly protest it was only one hand, he'll tell you to shut up and get on with the game. Very, very serious. When they talk to you, it's invariably with a very stern attitude. There were certain referees, years ago, who would give as good as they got. If you said: "Get your effing book out, ref" they'd simply tell you to eff off back. They don't do that now and some referees won't talk to you at all. It's very sad.

Professionals for professionals

There aren't enough quality referees about anyway now, compared to, say, ten years ago. I can understand why. They are under a lot of pressure on the pitch and some referees just don't need the hassle. The really annoying thing is that they all seem to have a different interpretation of the rules.

I think they should allow players to become referees when they retire, like cricketers are allowed to become umpires. It's possible now but it's a long process and by the time you've reached the top it's about time for you to retire.

They should cut a few corners and let ex-players become referees as soon as they finish playing. I think a lot of players would do it, especially if it was professional. It would be another way of staying in football. Referees will eventually have to become professional or at least semi-professional. It would benefit the game no end. If each club put money into a fund, pro rata, for a year it would create a kitty from which to pay them their wages and that would allow them to become at least semi-professional and to hold meetings and attend seminars on a regular basis.

If players bring the game into disrepute, we get brought up before the disciplinary committee, and sometimes before your own club as well, and you get done. You hardly ever hear of a referee being done. They can go back to their normal job.

We're professional footballers making a living out of the game, but for them it's a hobby, a bit of enjoyment. There's no real lasting pressure because they've got a job to go back to.

For the last ten or so years, the game has been going through problems with hooliganism which aren't as bad as they were, thankfully. People started looking for excuses, things to blame, and said that celebrations on the pitch incited the crowd. Now you don't even enjoy the thrill of scoring as much because referees stop you going to fans when you've scored. A lot of players like saluting the crowd. Scoring a goal is an unbelievably good feeling and you want to share it with the people who have come to see you score. Celebrating is part of the enjoyment of the game.

But I believe a a bad refereeing can create as much trouble as anything else. People never look at poor referees as a possible cause of trouble, though.

Missing, presumed surplus to requirements

Roger Wylde was the biggest micky-taker on the field. He had a lot of skill when he was a youngster. When he was at Oldham with Simon Stainrod, the pair of them used to see how many nutmegs they could each get in a game. At Sheffield Wednesday he used stand over the ball in front of a defender knocking his knees together, and was always willing to acknowledge the crowd while he was running. The crowd loved it but, predictably, Jack Charlton didn't and he knocked it out of him. It was a shame because it always got the crowd going, even if the score was 0-0 and it was a drab match.

Humour has gone out of the game a lot. Football is a lot more of a serious business than it was years and years ago. The characters have gone out of the game. I know it's a popular whinge, but it's true. Football is a serious business; it's big business and more serious because of it.

Everything is basically money-orientated.

A lot of players are driven out of the game because, although they are characters with bags if skill, they are not tremendously hard workers, which is what the modern day demand is for.

It's a high pressure game because of the financial implications and fitness is everything. It's a sorry state of affairs but it's going to get even worse. There was a lot more skill around years ago, but nowadays managers take on fit players and hard workers rather than those simply blessed with natural ability. A few years ago they might have said: "He's skilful but lacks a bit of pace and doesn't work hard enough, we'll take him for a couple of years and see how he progresses." Now they don't. They keep the hard workers and those with a tough attitude. It's playing a percentage game.

Coaches are taking flair out of the game. I'm guilty of it too. There was a little fellow in one of the summer soccer schools I run for kids and all he wanted to do was to take the ball round four or five other kids, which he was brilliant at. It was a pleasure to watch but I found myself telling him to try and pass the ball, stopping him from doing what he was very good at.

It starts from a very early age these days. It's very rare that you'll see anyone now with the skill of Jimmy Johnstone or Charlie Cooke. It's bad. I suppose the skill is coming back a bit more because more and more teams are trying to play with two wingers, who are now in demand. Good ones are very hard to find.

Making a point: Brighton defender Gary Chivers puts the finger on me.

Our ball: In an appealing mood against Manchester City.

Up against the wall: Kevin Hodges feels the force of a West Ham free kick.

Down but not out: Football can be a hard life.

Hair raising: Keeping things close to my chest, against Steve Terry again.

Ouch!: A tender moment against Stoke City.

Centre of attention: Mixing it in the Watford penalty area.

High kicks: Going in where it hurts with Phil King of Swindon Town.

16

THE FUTURE

AS I said at the beginning, football is the be all and end all of my life but no-one can play forever. I couldn't even play until I'm 42, like Tommy Hutchison.

Watching from the sidelines won't be easy either. Footballers are the worst spectators in the world because they know what is supposed to be happening when they look at the game. You tend to be very critical of games, even when they are on television.

The one thing I will miss most of all when I do eventually retire is the Saturday afternoon routine. Everything in your life is geared to Saturday afternoons. For the remainder of the week you're wrapped in cotton wool. By the time you retire, you've been pampered for such a long time it's a shock when suddenly you're on your own again. I've been told it's not until players have been finished for six months that they realise that's it, all over.

But your Saturday routine is still virtually the same if you're still in the game in a coaching or managerial capacity so that won't happen to me for a while yet. Hopefully I can hold down a permanent job in the game which I love so much.

People will forget. They forget very quickly. Plymouth people like and respect me because of what I've achieved at Argyle but there will a new hero two or three months after I've left. I realise that and I'm sure everyone else does. I'll pick up the paper and see that someone has banged in a few goals, when it used to be me. It's an instant thing. You've gone and within weeks it's not Tommy Tynan who is in the headlines but Owen Pickard or Paul Robinson or someone else. That's football.

One of the trainers at Sheffield Wednesday when I started out said strikers should always look at Sunday papers because you are successful at what you've set out to do if your name is in it. At the end of your career, all of a sudden that's taken away from you.

In Plymouth, people tend to remember their footballers with affection. I don't know why it should be the case but it is. Mike Bickle's still tremendously well thought of down here. He's always referred to as "Mike Bickle, who used to play for Argyle." When a footballer retires or even moves into management, he has got to become, for better or worse, an ordinary person, not a star, and that is probably difficult. Sometimes, it might be nice, but I've enjoyed the adulation and I will miss it when I do hang up my boots.

Managing by myself

There is only one quality for management and that's success. If you're a successful manager, you're a good manager. If you're a failure, you're a bad manager. There's managers about who are very good at doing certain things. Len Ashurst, for instance, is very good at coming to a club, sorting it out and bringing in a new system. He's a hard man, not the sort you could tell to eff off. But he's always treated his older players with respect because they've been through the mill. Two sets of values. Ken Brown would treat everyone the same.

I'm ruthless enough to be a manager and I'm single-minded enough to think that I could do it. I know I couldn't please all the people all the time and wouldn't twist myself into the ground trying. I might need someone as a second-in-command who could slow me down a bit because I can be a right bastard when I need to be. Football management is not just about picking eleven men for a match; there's a lot of man-management involved as well.

Managers don't get themselves sacked, players do. At the end of the day, whatever a manager tells you to do, come 3 pm he can't do a single thing except sit and watch. If you don't do what he wants and don't get the results, he gets the sack. Players don't get sacked. That sort of situation is enough to make you very wary about being a manager, though it's not enough to put me off altogether. As a player, I've always been employed, but I know lots of managers who've suddenly found themselves out of a job.

I've been in clubs when things aren't going well and because of it, the dressing rooms aren't good places to be in. When Newport were bottom of the league, Len Ashurst did something I've never understood. He split the dressing room up. All the lads he felt weren't doing it for the club or who didn't have the best interests of the club at heart were put in a dressing room on their own. It lasted two or three weeks. They trained on their own and weren't picked. At the time, he said: "I'll bring you back if you can prove in the next three weeks you've got the club's interests at heart and do well for the club" and eventually he did. Four of them came back and two were transferred.

It's the manager who gets the stick if things start going wrong all of a sudden. There's very few managers who stay in one job for a long time unless they are continuously successful. It's very unusual that managers keep their job for longer than three years.

Mind you, being a manager can be a pretty exasperating life. After Mick Prendergast was transferred from Sheffield Wednesday to Barnsley, he was playing in the reserves as a prelude to Saturday's first-team game when he picked up a little injury with half-an-hour to go. The manager phoned down to the dug out and said: ``Get him off, get the substitute on.'' The trainer replied: ``I can't.'' The manager said: ``Don't tell me you can't, just get the sub on.''

Ten minutes went by and Mick was starting to limp a bit so the 'phone rings again in the dug-out asking why the substitute hadn't been put on and ordering the trainer to get Mick off because he was needed on

Saturday. Another ten minutes went by and the manager had had enough, so he went down to the dug-out. Mick saw this happening and started walking across because obviously he thought he was finally going to be taken off. The manager shouted: ``Get Mick off, get the sub on.'' The trainer said: ``I can't.'' The manager said: ``Why not?'' He replied: ``I've sent him to get the fish and chips.'' The manager exploded and Mick shrugged his shoulders, turned round and carried on.

Often managers get to the stage where they don't believe they can achieve anything more with a certain set of players, which is why there are regular large turnovers of players every two or three years. I think Dave Smith reached the point at Plymouth where he believed he couldn't do any more with the players he had got, didn't have the resources to buy better players, and wanted out. That's why he went to Dundee.

I'm totally against the idea of women managers. It's hard enough for a player whose been in the game 20 years to get a manager's job. And I don't believe that anyone who hasn't played the game to a certain level could have enough knowledge to run a football club. I'm sure most managers in the Football League have played at some level of the professional game. That's the way it should be. Women have their own ideas about football and there's some very knowledgeable women about in football, but they have no experience. Certain women would say they could handle it but I don't think they could handle it at the top level.

Without a doubt, women are very valuable supporters. A lot of females get interested because their husbands or sons are interested and it's natural for them to take an interest as well. Young girls tend to go because they idolise some of the players, maybe the better looking ones. You get a lot of 13/14-year-old girls hanging round the ground, especially in the school holidays, watching you train, waiting for autographs, that sort of thing.

A few years ago, clubs tried female physiotherapists, but that has never really caught on. Outside the First Division it is important that a lot of club physios have played the game because they serve a dual purpose, acting as coaches or reserve team managers as well. Like Malcolm Musgrove does at Plymouth. It boils down to finances again.

A little application

I'm going to have a go at being a soccer manager. Whether I'm successful or not, I want to be able to say to myself that I had a go at it. I did it, if it doesn't work then, so, I'm a failure. It isn't nice but at least I've had a go. Whether I'm allowed to have a go or not is another matter.

I've seen too many managers come and go and do things I would not dream of doing. It's very black and white, the way I see it - although I know there's probably a lot of grey areas - and I want to see if they work. Being a soccer manager is something I want to do and I shall be very disappointed if I don't get the chance. I don't care if I'm on a hiding to nothing.

I'd like to see if I have the talent to manage that I believe I have. If I became a bit of a sod and failed as a a manager then at least I would have done it my way. I wouldn't like to come away from a a manager's job and think I'd been stabbed in the back or handled things wrongly.

I'd make mistakes, everyone does. We'll just have to wait and see. There's not a lot of managerial jobs about and it's a very risky business.

Every manager is different. I wouldn't be a kick and rush merchant; I'd have my team playing intelligent football. The most difficult thing for me being a manager would be the one-to-one situations in the dressing room because I'd probably blow my top too quickly. That's why I'd need a good second-in-command, someone to say: "Hang on, you're being a little too harsh there."

I've seen Dave Smith slaughter people without actually saying anything. Steve Cooper was either on real top form or completely abysmal, there were no half-measures with him. If he wasn't doing well Dave Smith would come into the dressing room and say: "You're not doing this" or "You should be doing that" and Stevie would have a go back at him, which was silly really because he was on a loser from the beginning.

In situations like that the manager is always right, even when he's wrong. I'd like to see if I could cope with it. I wouldn't want to do it if

I thought I wasn't capable. I'm sure I am capable but I'll never know unless I have a go.

I've learnt a lot of things in football. Colin Addison brought team spirit to Newport by having regular parties for the first three months he was there. Directors, officials, players and their wives were all invited, which was absolutely brilliant. Everyone went because there was a club fine if you didn't and at the end of the day it achieved the purpose of bringing the players and their wives together.

I'd go as far as to say I've learnt something from every manager I've played under. Len Ashurst was the most influential because, as I've said, he kicked me up the backside at a vital time and probably saved my career.

I've also learnt that it can be a precarious occupation. When Plymouth Argyle stayed up in Newcastle last season after an evening match at St James's Park, all the lads went out to a night-club afterwards for a drink.

We decided to leave in the wee small hours of the morning and went outside to hail a cab. I was stunned to recognise the driver. It was Bobby Moncur, who signed me when I originally joined Plymouth Argyle. Six years ago he was my manager, now he's driving cab in Newcastle. Smacks you in the face, doesn't it?

There are a lot of people in football who wouldn't make a manager or who wouldn't want to be a manager because they are good number twos. I might find that out myself while I'm learning my trade at Torquay, I don't know. I'll have to wait and see.

I applied for the Argyle manager's job when Dave Smith left for Dundee and the board sent a lovely letter back after the interview saying they didn't realise how ambitious I was and how much they'd enjoyed the interview. I was very pleased with the letter and I've still got it.

Applying for the Plymouth job provided a great insight into the mechanics of the boardroom. I was surprised because I thought I knew the directors and which ones would be asking all the questions. I was interviewed for about 40 minutes and about 80 per cent of the questions came from just one director, who I didn't even think would be there.

They were good enough to give me an interview. They could have just said they didn't think I was the right man for the job because I'd said all along that I wanted to continue playing and I don't think they fancied the idea of a player-manager.

Sitting down and listening to them was, as I said, a great insight. It was my first ever interview for a job so I thought I'd better take a little bit of advice. A friend of mine, Glyn Thomas, from D G Sports, in Plympton, who have been my sponsors, helped me out.

Glyn was involved in interviews when he was in the forces and he told me certain things you do and certain things you don't do in interviews, which was a great help. We talked about hand gestures and did an hour's session where he told me what interviewers actually look for and how they can tell when you're being honest and so on. I was so nervous before the interview but when I got in there I thought : "I know these people, I'll just be totally straight with them."

A lot of people thought that Ken Brown would be funny with me because I'd gone for the job, but he never even mentioned it. He didn't take the captaincy away from me - not until later anyway - which he could have done. I don't really know what he thought because he never said.

I didn't apply for the manager's job when Ken Brown was sacked, but not because I didn't want it or had changed my mind about becoming a manager. I was told early after they advertised the job that the directors were not prepared to take a chance on someone who had no experience of Football League management. I didn't want to waste the directors' time or mine by applying. Somewhere along the line, though, they obviously changed their mind because they opted for David Kemp, who had been a manager in Sweden but never in this country. Obviously, he'd more experience than I had and he's done a good job so far. There's no hard feelings.

Finishing thoughts

No disrespect to Torquay, but I did want to finish my playing career at Plymouth. I honestly didn't believe I would want to leave the area for another part of the country, which obviously hasn't been the case since I've signed for Torquay.

Gordon Nisbet wanted to do another year at Home Park and I believe that he should have done. If he'd been allowed to do that he would have retired and that would have been that. The same would have applied to me.

Outside the game, I've always fancied running a pub or a business, which is why I've been on business courses and pub management courses. But I'd like to stay in football indefinitely which is why I was very interested when Torquay offered me a coaching job.

I love football. You get fame from football if you do the right things. Everyone wants to be famous. I hate people who say that they don't want a big house or lots of money or to be famous. What a load of rubbish.

If I can get the biggest house in the world, make as much money as anyone else in the world and be as famous as anyone else in the world then why not? That's being ambitious.

I want a big house and plenty of money. I'm quite well-known, especially in the Westcountry, where I'm quite a name. I must say I'm quite surprised how well known I actually am, but I won't be surprised when people forget me after I've finished playing. Sad, maybe, but not surprised.

17

THE BEST OF TEAMS

FOOTBALL IS a game of opinions and people are always asking me "Who is the best player you've played with in your career?" or "Which Plymouth Argyle players have you rated?"or "Who are the best players in the Football League?" so, just for a bit of fun, I've sat down and selected some hypothetical sides that might help answer those questions and others.

Argyle elite

I'll start by choosing an imaginary Plymouth Argyle side from players that I've played with during my time at Home Park. It's purely my choice and isn't meant to be a criticism of any of the managers who I've played under.

In goal, it would have to be Rhys Wilmot. On his day, I don't think there are many better goalkeepers in the Second Division, or in football as a whole. Alan Miller had a great spell down here when he was on loan from Arsenal but he has not proved himself yet. He has got tremendous potential, but that's all it is at the moment, potential. I've seen many players with potential who've failed to make the grade. Steve Cherry is a good goalkeeper too, but after playing with Rhys I would have to say that he is the better all-round 'keeper. Like I say, on his day, he's one of the best six goalkeepers in the country.

Gordon Nisbet would be right-back, no doubt whatsoever. Simply, I haven't played with a better right-back at Plymouth than Nissie, and that is not being disrespectful to Kenny Brown or any of the others.

The left-back spot would go to Leigh Cooper. Not just because he's a friend and he's still at the club but because I honestly don't think there's been many better left-backs at the club. Moving to that position from midfield was the best thing that happened in his career. Dave Smith moved him to left-back and all of a sudden people started talking about him.

Centre-backs are the most difficult of all to chose. I had to make a hard decision, but in the end I went for Adrian Burrows and Mark Smith. Shades has matured into a very good central defender after a settling-in year. He's very quick, not many people beat him, and over 40-odd games he gives a really good solid performance, although he's prone to one or two lapses of concentration every now and again. Shades will always have a couple of off-games during a season; when he does, they're normally absolute nightmares.

Smudger is simply a class defender and he eventually won the vote over Gerry McElhinney. I knew him when I was at Sheffield Wednesday - he used to clean my boots then! - and he's impressed me ever since.

A lot of people will be surprised I haven't picked Lindsay Smith because he was a good mate as well as a good defender, and I did toy with that idea.

I would definitely play Garry Nelson up front with me, even though I only played ten games with him on loan from Rotherham. He wanted to play up front all the time, but Dave Smith preferred him on the left-wing and, having said he's a great front-man, he's still a hell of a left-winger. I think he proved to everyone he could score goals when he joined Brighton.

Len Ashurst, at Newport, said if you picked a side and didn't include yourself then you wanted shooting, because it showed you had no confidence in yourself. That's why I've picked myself. Len would occasionally get all the players at Newport to individually select what they thought was the best possible team was and some of the players actually left themselves out.

Maybe they were looking at it too objectively but Len learnt a lot from their attitude. If a player is fighting for a position at a club and thinks someone is better than him, he's going to think that all the time. If he's pushing to get into the team and he thinks the fellow already in the team is better than him, what chance has he got of believing he can make the side? I always think I can score goals and I think my record proves that I can.

I would pick Gordon Staniforth and give him a free attacking role. Gordon's best games were when he played off me and played wide. He was one of the few players I've ever played with when I knew what they were going to do all the time. He'd go past a defender and whip the ball in and that was his job done.

The central midfield was very difficult to select but I settled on John Matthews and Kevin Summerfield. It's ironic really. Two players who cost the club nothing benefited Argyle hugely for four or five years. They came on free transfers and have been very good servants of the club. What Matty did for the club was tremendous, his passing ability is second to none.

Kevin Summerfield is a very slightly-built person but he's quick, can put his foot on the ball and is a good finisher. To be honest, I'm surprised he doesn't score more goals than he does. We missed him when he broke his leg. I've always thought his best position is not either midfield or striker but somewhere in-between, sitting behind the front two and given a free role, not to mark, but to get forward as much as possible.

I was tempted to pick Russell Coughlin as well but I'm picking a team, not just 11 names. If I was a manager and Russ became available, I'd buy him. A lot of people said he didn't like tackling, but I don't believe that because I've seen him go in for all sorts of tackles. He didn't like what Dave Smith tried to get him to do; he'd like all players to get forward as much as possible when the ball was up and back as much as possible when we were defending, but Russ and Matty just liked to sit in midfield and pass the ball, which is what they were good at.

Apart from Leigh, Plymouth have lacked a natural left-sided midfielder over the years, but I'd pick Nicky Marker to fulfil the role in my Argyle team. It's funny that a central defender who was bought by Dave Smith to be a right-back has shown that he can serve Plymouth well on the left side of midfield, even if he does prefer to play defence.

Nicky's probably one of the best players Argyle have got at the moment. He's young, he's learning, getting better every match, and various other clubs are looking at him enviously, which doesn't surprise me in the least.

There are a few players who I would have liked to pick but who just missed out. John Clayton didn't get much of a run in the team when I was here, because I took his place in the side, but he did prove that, given the right service, he could get goals. Andy Rogers was another player who, when he was on song, was absolutely brilliant, and Kevin Hodges was in a different class for two seasons.

So my final selection would be: 1 Rhys Wilmot, 2 Gordon Nisbet, 3 Leigh Cooper, 4 John Matthews, 5 Adrian Burrows, 6 Mark Smith, 7 Gordon Staniforth, 8 Kevin Summerfield, 9 Tommy Tynan, 10 Garry Nelson, 11 Nicky Marker. Subs: John Clayton, Kevin Hodges.

By my side

Spreading the net a little wider, I've chosen a side out of all the players I've played with at the various clubs I've been at, remembering them at the peak of their careers.

The choice of goalkeeper was difficult. I rate Rhys Wilmot very highly and believe he will play in the First Division one day. His performances on the field have been outstanding, plus he's a nice lad and gets on well with everyone. But I've gone for Chris Turner, who I played with at Sheffield Wednesday. Chris has proved himself by playing for various clubs, including Manchester United and Sheffield Wednesday in the First Division, and Rhys has yet to do that. But it was a tight choice.

The right-back is still Nissie. Like me, he probably had his best years in the later part of his career and even when he left Plymouth he was probably one of the best players in the Second Division. A lot of people have said that Kevin Hodges never recovered from the loss of the service Nissie gave him on the right. Nissie was fit lad and got forward well to support Kevin, and they had a good understanding.

Leigh Cooper is left-back again. He is simply the best left-back I've played with. He can go through 46 games a season and never be outstanding, but is tremendously consistent, probably the most consistent player I've known in my career. He's quick and not easily beaten. If you asked the manager to rate his performance every match out of ten, he'd never get a nine, but he'd never get a six either. Always a seven or an eight.

The two centre-backs again proved a hard choice to make, because they are the lynch-pin of any side. Ronnie Moran at Liverpool said that if the two central defenders are doing their job and not much is getting past them, then it eases the rest of the side. If you look like you're not going to give anything away, you always feel capable of winning games. Outside the First Division, there are not many exceptional centre-backs, just the odd one or two.

One of the centre-backs would have to be Keith Oakes. All the big clubs took a look at him when he was at Newport and I'm still surprised he never moved on to better things. He never even played in the Second Division. He was a great up-and-down centre-half, a good stopper and had good ball control. He was a big lad but wasn't just a stopper. Maybe the only criticism against him is that he lacked a little bit of pace.

The other would be Kenny Stroud, another Newport team-mate, although he was probably more of a midfielder. I played against him when he moved to Bristol City, so I know from personal experience what he's capable of.

In midfield, I'd put Nigel Vaughan on the left and Steve Lowndes on the right. Both are Welsh lads and both are very quick, especially Nigel. The service John Aldridge and I got from them at Newport was unbelievable and they got more than 25 goals between them in one season together, which from midfield is excellent.

I'd pick John Aldridge to play alongside me up front. We had a great understanding at Newport and went through one magical spell when neither of us could do anything wrong. If he wasn't scoring then I was, and if I wasn't scoring then he was. For one season, everything went perfectly. I was just disappointed we didn't play more than one whole season together. He has everything a central forward needs; he is good in the air, very quick, and an excellent finisher. You can't argue with that or with his record, which speaks for itself.

John Aldridge came to Newport from South Liverpool and struggled for his first couple of seasons. He nearly went to Tranmere for £10,00 just before Len Ashurst got the sack, because he and his wife were homesick, and he had actually arranged a month's loan.

He found it hard to adjust from non-league football to playing every day but he eventually got his act together and proved what he could do.

One thing I'm very sorry about is that we didn't play together more often. We had a good understanding. He was the runner and I was the target man and everything just seemed to fall for us. If I wasn't scoring, he was and vice versa.

People have said Argyle should have signed John as well. At the time, we were the best striking pair in the lower divisions. There was a bid from a northern club of £180,000 for the pair of us which was turned down. That would have kept Newport in clover for the next five years. As it is, we've gone on to better things and they've folded. It's sad, but it's one of those things.

I was indirectly involved in certain things and I know John would have moved to Plymouth if the situation had been up and running, but there were one or two things in the boardroom that weren't quite right at the time.

I think that's one of the reasons why Bobby Moncur left. It's not that he didn't want Aldridge, just that it wasn't totally his own choice. More a boardroom decision than his own decision.

The other forward would be Gordon Hobson, who was always scoring goals for Lincoln. Left on his own up front he would have been an even better footballer than he is. He was too old when he moved to the First Division with Southampton. When he was in his mid-twenties, he was in a different class.

In midfield, I'd have another player who left Lincoln and ended up playing for Southampton, proving he had what it takes at the highest level, and that is Glenn Cockerill.

On the substitutes bench, I'd go for Garry Nelson - I rate him very highly - and John Matthews, ever the dependable choice. I might even be tempted to have Gordon Hobson starting on the bench and Matty sitting in midfield, depending on whether I wanted an attacking formation or a more defensive one.

So my final selection is: 1 Chris Turner (Sheffield Wednesday), 2 Gordon Nisbet (Plymouth Argyle), 3 Leigh Cooper (Plymouth Argyle), 4 Steve Lowndes (Newport County), 5 Keith Oakes (Newport County), 6 Kenny Stroud (Newport County), 7 Glenn Cockerill (Lincoln City), 8 Gordon Hobson (Lincoln City), 9 Tommy Tynan, 10 John Aldridge (Newport County), 11 Nigel Vaughan (Newport County). Subs: Garry Nelson (Plymouth Argyle), John Matthews (Plymouth Argyle).

A dream team

The next selection is every manager's dream - or nightmare, depending on which way you look at it: picking a team from every single player in the Football League.

I still don't think there's a better goalkeeper in the league than Peter Shilton, even though he's 40. He makes very few errors and is very consistent. Neville Southall pushed him hard for my selection, but the only difficulty I would have had in picking the goalkeeper would be if Gordon Banks was still playing!

Steve Nicol is probably a better right-back than a midfielder, which is where I'd originally thought about playing him. But he can play anywhere and is a dream of a player to have in any side.

At left-back, I'd have Stuart Pearce. I know he's got his critics and that some of his tackles are a little high or a little late, but he is an unbelievable ball-winner and gets forward well.

Alan Hansen strolls into the side at centre-back. He is one of the best footballers in the league, so relaxed on the ball and off it as well. In some of the games I've seen him play, he doesn't even appear to break sweat, just floats through the game. Different class.

Hansen's partner is Bryan Robson, the most obvious choice in a less than obvious position. Ask a lot of players in the game and they'll tell you he should have been playing there for England for years. I hope that's what will happen after the World Cup. He's getting on, but at his best is the best player in the entire Football League; captain of England and the most consistent player for club and country over the last ten years.

In midfield, John Barnes and and Steve McMahon go on the team-sheet without too much hesitation. They make Liverpool tick. McMahon is like Robson, a good tackler and a good leader. He has got fitness, a lot of aggression and skill, and loves to get forward to score goals. His heart is enormous.

Barnes is a different class on the ball and has got everything that a footballer wants except, perhaps, consistency. At Watford, he was a bit of an enigma but at Liverpool he produces his flashes of skill more often, possibly because they want more from him and have worked out the best way to get it. He's working harder now than he has ever had to, and when you're working hard you're always going to be involved in the game. When I say working harder, I don't just mean running around like a headless chicken, but closing down players when you haven't got the ball and taking players on when you have. It's what Liverpool expect.

There aren't two better strikers in the league than Mark Hughes and Ian Rush, so I've reluctantly left myself out! I don't even make the bench in this team! Rushie had a bad time after coming back from Italy but he is still the most clinical finisher in British football. I never realised how much work he got through off the ball before I watched him closely one game. He'd be walking about one minute and the next he was running back, putting four defenders under pressure, one after the other. He's always chasing back trying to win the ball. When he's scored a hat-trick, you forget about the other part of his game. And to be honest, he plays up front virtually on his own, which is very difficult to do.

Mark Hughes probably doesn't score enough goals. When you look at his record he's not exactly prolific, but he's strong, quick and aggressive and does score some truly great goals. With Rush, he forms a great strike force and I find it hard to believe they haven't really hit it off together for Wales.

I've put David Rocastle in the middle of midfield because he can score goals and has got skill and pace, and alongside him I've stuck my neck out, cheated a little, and gone for Liam Brady, even though he's officially retired. He's unbelievable, the way he can make space and use it. He's always got time on the ball. When Plymouth played at Upton Park last season, I can't remember him giving the ball away in the entire 90 minutes. That says everything about him. Even at his age, he's still capable of running a game.

The substitutes, the ones that nearly made it, would be Southall, Gary Lineker, Paul Gascoigne, Neil Webb and Dave Watson, who is probably a bit of a surprise selection, but he's a good centre-half, very strong in the air and not many people I've played against have shut me out of a game so comprehensively.

My final Football League XI is: 1 Peter Shilton (Derby County), 2 Steve Nicol (Liverpool), 3 Stuart Pearce (Nottingham Forest), 4 Steve McMahon (Liverpool), 5 Bryan Robson (Manchester United), 6 Alan Hansen (Liverpool), 7 David Rocastle (Arsenal), 8 Liam Brady (West Ham United), 9 Ian Rush (Liverpool), 10 Mark Hughes (Manchester United), 11 John Barnes (Liverpool). Subs: Neville Southall (Everton), Dave Watson (Everton), Neil Webb (Manchester United), Paul Gascoigne (Tottenham Hotspur), Gary Lineker (Tottenham Hotspur).

Bar none

Now for a real bit of fun. The final side is the sociable side, and that means general sociability, not just being a great drinker, and it would be: 1 Geoff Crudgington (Plymouth Argyle), 2 Jimmy Mullen (Sheffield

Wednesday), 3 Leigh Cooper (Plymouth Argyle), 4 John Matthews (Plymouth Argyle), 5 Gerry McElhinney (Plymouth Argyle), 6 Hugh Dowd (Sheffield Wednesday), 7 Russell Coughlin (Plymouth Argyle), 8 John Clayton (Plymouth Argyle), 9 Tommy Tynan, 10 John Aldridge (Newport County), 11 Gordon Staniforth (Plymouth Argyle). Subs: Rhys Wilmot, Kenny Brown, David Byrne, Sean McCarthy, Mark Stuart (all Plymouth Argyle).

Leigh is one of the boys, always likes going out, and Gerry and Hugh are both Irish lads, which might or might not be the reason for their affability. Hughie liked his Guinness and Gerry always made sure the lads were well looked after when he was captain of Plymouth. I'm sure that one of the reason the team did so well under him was because he led off the field as well as on it.

Clayts is a very sociable lad and was the first to join in a drink, but the last to buy the round, and John Aldridge is still one of the lads even now. He and his wife, Joan love the social occasions. Stanny loved a joke and a drink but had this habit of going missing when we were on a night out. He knew when he'd had enough and when he reached that stage he'd just go home. We've all been out on occasions and looked round for Stanny, only to find that he and his wife have just gone home, without saying goodbye or anything. He's had enough and doesn't want to be too embarrassing and that's okay.

The subs are all part of Plymouth's Crazy Gang. You can imagine how they got that title. They are all high-spirited young men who aren't afraid to express themselves when they go out for enjoyment. As I said earlier, I've found the sponsored plates from my car lying all over Plymouth after they've enjoyed a night out and come across the car during the evening.

Enjoying the life that football gives you is important and these people enjoy life and, at times, have helped me enjoy my life. That's it in a nutshell, really.

STATISTICAL BREAKDOWN

THOMAS EDWARD TYNAN
Born: Liverpool, Merseyside, November 17, 1955.

APPEARANCES GOALS

1975/76 SWANSEA CITY (loan)
Football League:

1	v Doncaster Rovers a	L	1-2	1
2	v Darlington h	W	2-0	
3	v Bradford City h	W	3-1	1
4	v Barnsley a	D	0-0	
5	v Reading a	L	0-1	
6	v Torquay United h	W	3-0	

Total: 6 appearances, 2 goals

1976/77 SHEFFIELD WEDNESDAY
Football League:

7	v Swindon Town a	L	2-5	1
8	v Chesterfield h	W	4-1	1
9	v Wrexham a	D	2-2	
10	v Lincoln City a	D	1-1	
11	v Chester City h	W	3-0	1
12	v Gillingham h	W	2-0	
13	v Reading a	W	1-0	
14	v Shrewsbury Town h	L	0-1	
15	v Rotherham United h	L	1-3	
16	v Bury a	W	3-1	2
17	v Crystal Palace h	W	1-0	
18	v Peterborough United a	W	2-1	2
19	v Tranmere Rovers h	W	3-1	
20	v Oxford United a	D	1-1	1
21	v York City h	W	3-2	1
22	v Grimsby Town a	D	1-1	
23	v Brighton & Hove Albion h	D	0-0	
24	v Mansfield Town a	L	0-1	
25	v Northampton Town a	W	2-0	
26	v Walsall a	L	1-5	
27	v Bury h	W	1-0	
28	v Port Vale h	L	1-2	
29	v Portsmouth a	W	3-0	2
30	v Chester a	L	0-1	
31	v Swindon Town h	W	3-1	
32	v Chesterfield a	L	0-2	
33	v Wrexham h	W	3-1	
34	v Lincoln City h	D	1-1	
35	v Gillingham a	L	0-1	
36	v Reading h	W	2-1	
37	v Shrewsbury Town a	D	1-1	
38	v York City a	W	2-0	1
39	v Rotherham United a	W	1-0	
40	v Preston North End h	W	1-0	1
41	v Crystal Palace a	L	0-4	
42	v Peterborough United h	W	4-0	
43	v Brighton & Hove Albion a	L	2-3	
44	v Tranmere Rovers a	L	0-1	
45	v Oxford United h	W	2-0	1

Total: 39 appearances, 14 goals.

FA Cup:

1	v Stockport County h	W	2-0	1
2	v Darlington a	L	0-1	

Total: 2 appearances, 1 goal.

Football League Cup:

1	v Watford h	W	3-1	
2	v Millwall a	L	0-3	

Total: 2 appearances.

1977/78 SHEFFIELD WEDNESDAY
Football League:

46	v Swindon Town h	D	1-1	1
47	v Walsall h	D	0-0	
48	v Bury a	L	0-3	
49	v Shrewsbury Town h	L	0-1	
50	v Chester a	L	1-2	1
51	v Port Vale a	D	0-0	
52	v Peterborough United h	L	0-1	
53	v Portsmouth a	D	2-2	1
54	v Preston North End a	L	1-2	
55	v Chesterfield h	W	1-0	1
56	v Exeter City a	L	1-2	
57	v Wrexham a	D	1-1	1
58	v Lincoln City h	W	2-0	
59	v Bradford City a	L	2-3	1
60	v Carlisle United h	W	3-1	1
61	v Oxford United a	L	0-1	
62	v Gillingham h	D	0-0	
63	v Colchester United h	L	1-2	
64	v Cambridge United a	L	0-3	
65	v Tranmere Rovers a	L	1-3	1
66	v Rotherham United h	W	1-0	
67	v Hereford United h	W	1-0	
68	v Carlisle United a	L	0-1	
69	v Swindon Town a	D	2-2	
70	v Exeter City h	W	2-1	
71	v Bury h	W	3-2	1
72	v Port Vale h	W	3-1	1
73	v Peterborough United a	L	1-2	
74	v Portsmouth h	D	0-0	
75	v Shrewsbury Town a	D	0-0	
76	v Chesterfield a	D	2-2	1
77	v Chester h	D	1-1	
78	v Lincoln City a	L	1-3	
79	v Bradford City h	W	2-0	1

80 v Rotherham United a	W	2-1	
81 v Tranmere Rovers h	W	1-0	1
82 v Hereford United a	W	1-0	
83 v Plymouth Argyle a	D	1-1	
84 v Oxford United h	W	2-1	
85 v Gillingham a	L	1-2	
86 v Preston North End h	W	1-0	1
87 v Cambridge United h	D	0-0	
88 v Walsall a	D	1-1	1
89 v Wrexham h	W	2-1	1

Total: 44 appearances, 16 goals.

FA Cup:

3 v Bury h	W	1-0	
4 v Wigan Athletic a	L	0-1	

Total: 2 appearances.

Football League Cup:

3 v Doncaster Rovers h	W	5-2	
4 v Doncaster Rovers a	W	3-0	1
5 v Blackpool a	D	2-2	1
6 v Blackpool h	W	3-1	1
7 v Walsall h	W	2-1	1
8 v Everton h	L	1-3	1

Total: 6 appearances, 5 goals.

1978/79 SHEFFIELD WEDNESDAY

Football League:

90 v Peterborough United a	L	0-2	
91 v Colchester United h	D	0-0	
92 v Lincoln City a	W	2-1	1
93 v Southend United h	W	3-2	
94 v Gillingham a	D	0-0	
95 v Mansfield Town a	D	1-1	
96 v Plymouth Argyle h	L	2-3	
97 v Bury h	D	0-0	

Total: 8 appearances, 1 goal.

Football League Cup:

9 v Doncaster Rovers a	W	1-0	
10 v Doncaster Rovers h	L	0-1	
11 v Doncaster Rovers a	W	1-0	
12 v Aston Villa a	L	0-1	

Total: 4 appearances.

1978/79 LINCOLN CITY

Football League:

98 v Colchester United h	D	0-0	
99 v Gillingham a	L	2-4	
100 v Swindon Town h	L	0-3	
101 v Mansfield Town h	L	0-1	
102 v Sheffield Wednesday a	D	0-0	
103 v Plymouth Argyle h	D	3-3	
104 v Oxford United h	D	2-2	1
105 v Chesterfield h	L	0-1	
106 v Peterborough United a	W	1-0	

Total: 9 appearances, 1 goal.

1978/79 NEWPORT COUNTY

Football League:

107 v Huddersfield Town a	W	1-0	
108 v Bradford City h	L	2-4	1
109 v Doncaster Rovers h	W	3-0	1
110 v Wimbledon a	D	0-0	
111 v Barnsley a	L	0-1	
112 v Crewe Alexandra a	W	1-0	1
113 v Northampton Town h	W	2-1	
114 v York City a	W	2-1	1
115 v Aldershot a	W	3-2	1
116 v Halifax Town h	W	2-0	
117 v Darlington a	L	0-1	
118 v Hereford United h	W	4-1	
119 v Torquay United a	L	0-2	
120 v Portsmouth h	W	1-0	
121 v Scunthorpe United h	W	2-0	
122 v Port Vale a	D	1-1	1
123 v Rochdale a	L	0-1	
124 v Grimsby Town h	D	1-1	
125 v AFC Bournemouth	W	2-0	1
126 v Halifax Town a	W	2-1	

Total: 20 appearances, 7 goals.

1979/80 NEWPORT COUNTY

Football League:

127 v Port Vale h	W	2-1	
128 v Aldershot a	W	1-0	
129 v AFC Bournemouth a	L	2-3	
130 v York City h	W	2-0	
131 v Huddersfield Town a	L	1-2	
132 v Bradford City h	L	1-2	
133 v Northampton Town h	W	2-1	1
134 v Doncaster Rovers a	W	3-1	1
135 v Lincoln City h	D	1-1	
136 v Northampton Town a	L	2-3	
137 v Halifax Town a	L	1-2	
138 v Wigan Athletic h	W	3-2	2
139 v Port Vale a	L	0-2	
140 v Portsmouth h	W	4-3	2
141 v Crewe Alexandra h	D	1-1	
142 v Stockport County a	W	5-0	
143 v Darlington h	W	4-0	
144 v Hartlepool United a	D	0-0	
145 v Scunthorpe United h	W	2-1	
146 v Peterborough United h	D	1-1	1

147 v Torquay United a	L	0-2	
148 v Walsall h	L	0-1	
149 v Hereford United h	W	1-0	
150 v York City a	L	1-2	
151 v AFC Bournemouth h	D	0-0	
152 v Lincoln City a	L	1-2	
153 v Doncaster Rovers h	W	2-1	
154 v Wigan Athletic a	W	1-0	
155 v Halifax Town h	W	5-2	
156 v Stockport County h	W	3-1	
157 v Peterborough United a	W	1-0	
158 v Rochdale h	W	1-0	
159 v Rochdale a	L	0-2	
160 v Walsall a	W	4-2	1

Total: 34 appearances, 8 goals.

<u>FA Cup:</u>

5 v Portsmouth a	L	0-1	

Total: 1 appearance.

<u>Football League Cup:</u>

13 v Plymouth Argyle h	W	1-0	1
14 v Plymouth Argyle a	L	0-2	

Total: 2 appearances, 1 goal.

1980/81 NEWPORT COUNTY

<u>Football League:</u>

161 v Burnley a	D	1-1	
162 v Charlton Athletic h	L	1-2	1
163 v Millwall h	W	2-1	2(2p)
164 v Carlisle United a	W	4-1	
165 v Gillingham a	L	2-3	
166 v Oxford United h	L	0-1	
167 v Chesterfield a	L	2-3	1
168 v Plymouth Argyle h	L	0-2	
169 v Brentford a	W	1-0	
170 v Reading h	D	0-0	
171 v Portsmouth h	W	2-1	
172 v Sheffield United a	L	0-2	
173 v Walsall a	L	0-1	
174 v Huddersfield Town h	W	3-2	
175 v Fulham h	W	2-1	
176 v Blackpool a	W	4-2	
177 v Hull City h	W	4-0	
178 v Charlton Athletic a	L	0-3	
179 v Burnley h	L	1-2	1(p)
180 v Rotherham United a	L	0-1	
181 v Chester a	D	1-1	
182 v Barnsley h	D	0-0	
183 v Chester h	D	1-1	
184 v Colchester United a	L	0-1	
185 v Swindon Town h	L	0-2	
186 v Exeter City a	D	2-2	1(p)
187 v Sheffield United h	W	4-0	1
188 v Huddersfield Town a	L	1-4	
189 v Rotherham United h	L	0-1	
190 v Millwall a	D	0-0	
191 v Oxford United a	W	1-0	
192 v Gillingham h	D	1-1	
193 v Reading a	D	1-1	
194 v Plymouth Argyle a	L	2-3	1
195 v Chesterfield h	W	5-1	2
196 v Brentford h	D	1-1	1
197 v Portsmouth a	D	0-0	
198 v Fulham a	L	1-2	
199 v Walsall h	D	1-1	
200 v Exeter City h	W	2-1	1
201 v Swindon Town a	D	1-1	
202 v Colchester United h	W	1-0	
203 v Barnsley a	L	1-4	
204 v Carlisle United h	W	4-0	1
205 v Hull City a	L	1-3	

Total: 45 appearances, 13 goals (4 penalties).

<u>FA Cup:</u>

6 v Plymouth Argyle a	L	0-2	

Total: 1 appearance.

<u>Football League Cup:</u>

15 v Hereford United a	L	0-1	
16 v Hereford United h	W	5-0	2
17 v Notts County h	D	1-1	
18 v Notts County a	L	0-2	

Total: 4 appearances, 2 goals.

<u>European Cup-Winners Cup:</u>

1 v Crusaders h	W	4-0	
2 v Crusaders a	D	0-0	
3 v Haugar h	W	6-0	2
4 v Carl Zeiss Jena a	D	2-2	2
5 v Carl Zeiss Jena h	L	0-1	

Total: 5 appearances, 4 goals.

1981/82 NEWPORT COUNTY

<u>Football League:</u>

206 v Southend United a	W	4-0	1
207 v Bristol City a	L	1-2	
208 v Preston North End h	D	1-1	
209 v Brentford h	L	0-1	
210 v Lincoln City a	D	2-2	2
211 v Doncaster Rovers h	W	1-0	
212 v Fulham a	L	1-3	1
213 v Millwall h	D	1-1	

214 v Portsmouth a	D	0-0	
215 v Walsall a	L	1-3	
216 v Plymouth Argyle h	L	0-1	
217 v Exeter City h	D	1-1	
218 v Wimbledon a	W	3-2	1
219 v Gillingham a	D	1-1	
220 v Reading h	W	3-1	
221 v Burnley a	L	1-2	
222 v Chesterfield a	L	0-1	
223 v Bristol City h	D	1-1	
224 v Oxford United a	D	1-1	1(p)
225 v Lincoln City h	D	0-0	
226 v Brentford a	L	0-2	
227 v Doncaster Rovers a	W	2-0	
228 v Portsmouth h	D	1-1	
229 v Bristol Rovers h	D	1-1	1 (p)
230 v Carlisle United a	D	2-2	1
231 v Walsall h	D	2-2	1
232 v Huddersfield Town a	L	0-2	
233 v Plymouth Argyle a	W	2-1	
234 v Chester a	W	2-0	
235 v Gillingham h	W	4-2	1 (p)
236 v Wimbledon h	D	0-0	
237 v Exeter City a	L	0-1	
238 v Burnley h	D	0-0	
239 v Preston North End a	L	1-2	
240 v Swindon Town a	D	1-1	
241 v Southend United h	W	3-2	2(1p)
242 v Huddersfield Town h	W	1-0	
243 v Swindon Town h	W	1-0	1(p)

Total: 38 appearances, 13 goals (5 penalties).

<u>FA Cup:</u>

7 v Colchester United a	L	0-2	

Total: 1 appearance.

<u>Football League Cup:</u>

19 v Torquay United h	D	0-0	
20 v Oldham Athletic a	L	0-1	

Total: 2 appearances.

<u>Football League Group Cup:</u>

1 v Torquay United h	D	0-0	
2 v Plymouth Argyle h	W	2-1	
3 v AFC Bournemouth a	D	0-0	
4 v Grimsby Town h	L	0-2	

Total: 4 appearances.

1982/83 NEWPORT COUNTY

<u>Football League:</u>

244 v Doncaster Rovers a	D	0-0	
245 v Chesterfield h	W	1-0	1
246 v Plymouth Argyle h	D	2-2	1
247 v Bradford City a	L	2-4	1
248 v Huddersfield Town h	W	2-1	
249 v Portsmouth a	W	2-1	
250 v Brentford a	L	0-2	
251 v Lincoln City h	W	1-0	1
252 v Bristol Rovers h	W	2-0	1
253 v Orient a	W	5-1	2
254 v Preston North End a	D	0-0	
255 v Southend United h	D	1-1	
256 v Wigan Athletic a	W	1-0	
257 v Sheffield United h	W	3-1	1
258 v Reading a	L	2-4	1(p)
259 v AFC Bournemouth h	W	5-1	
260 v Wrexham a	L	0-1	
261 v Gillingham h	W	2-1	
262 v Walsall h	D	1-1	
263 v Cardiff City a	L	2-3	
264 v Oxford United h	L	1-2	1
265 v Exeter City a	W	1-0	
266 v Millwall h	D	2-2	
267 v Doncaster Rovers h	L	1-2	
268 v Plymouth Argyle a	W	4-2	2
269 v Bradford City h	D	1-1	
270 v Chesterfield a	L	1-3	1
271 v Brentford h	D	0-0	
272 v Preston North End h	W	3-0	2(1p)
273 v Bristol Rovers a	W	3-1	2(1p)
274 v Orient h	W	4-1	
275 v Sheffield United a	L	0-2	
276 v Southend United a	W	4-1	
277 v Wigan Athletic h	W	1-0	
278 v Reading h	W	1-0	1
279 v Lincoln City a	W	4-1	2
280 v AFC Bournemouth a	W	1-0	
281 v Oxford United a	W	3-0	1
282 v Cardiff City h	W	1-0	
283 v Gillingham a	L	0-2	
284 v Portsmouth h	L	0-3	
285 v Walsall a	L	1-2	1(p)
286 v Wrexham h	W	4-0	3(1p)
287 v Millwall a	L	0-3	
288 v Huddersfield Town a	L	0-1	
289 v Exeter City h	D	1-1	

Total: 46 appearances, 25 goals (5 penalties)

FA Cup:

8 v Enfield a	D	0-0	
9 v Enfield h	W	4-2	3(1p)
10 v Orient h	W	1-0	1(p)
11 v Everton h	D	1-1	
12 v Everton a	L	1-2	

Total: 5 appearances, 4 goals (2 penalties).

Milk Cup:

21 v Exeter City a	W	2-1	
22 v Exeter City h	W	6-0	1
23 v Everton h	L	0-2	
24 v Everton a	D	2-2	1

Total: 4 appearances, 2 goals.

Football League Trophy:

5 v Torquay United h	L	0-1	
6 v Exeter City h	W	5-1	1
7 v Bristol City a	W	4-1	1
8 v Chester a	D	0-0	

Total: 4 appearances, 2 goals.
(NB: Details of Welsh Cup appearances (13) and goals (5) are omitted due to lack of data)

1983/84 PLYMOUTH ARGYLE
Football League:

290 v Wigan Athletic h	D	0-0	
291 v Millwall a	L	0-1	
292 v Rotherham United a	L	0-2	
293 v Gillingham h	D	1-1	
294 v Lincoln City a	L	1-3	1
295 v Preston North End h	W	1-0	
296 v Scunthorpe United h	W	4-0	
297 v Burnley a	L	1-2	
298 v AFC Bournemouth a	L	1-2	
299 v Oxford United h	W	2-1	
300 v Bristol Rovers h	D	1-1	
301 v Hull City a	W	2-1	1
302 v Sheffield United h	L	0-1	
303 v Port Vale a	W	1-0	
304 v Brentford a	D	2-2	1
305 v Bolton Wanderers h	W	2-0	
306 v Bradford City a	L	0-2	
307 v Southend United h	W	4-0	1(p)
308 v Walsall a	L	2-3	1
309 v Lincoln City h	D	2-2	
310 v Port Vale h	W	3-0	2
311 v Hull City h	W	2-0	1(p)
312 v Sheffield United a	L	0-2	
313 v Bristol Rovers a	L	0-2	
314 v Brentford h	D	1-1	
315 v AFC Bournemouth h	W	1-0	
316 v Millwall h	L	0-1	
317 v Oxford United a	L	0-5	
318 v Rotherham United h	D	1-1	1
319 v Wigan Athletic a	D	1-1	1
320 v Scunthorpe United a	L	0-3	
321 v Wimbledon h	L	1-2	1(p)
322 v Bolton Wanderers a	L	1-2	1(p)
323 v Newport County h	L	0-1	
324 v Exeter City a	D	1-1	

Total: 35 appearances, 12 goals (4 penalties).

FA Cup:

13 v Southend United a	D	0-0	
14 v Southend United h	W	2-0	1
15 v Barking h	W	2-1	
16 v Newport County h	D	2-2	1
17 v Newport County a	W	1-0	
18 v Darlington h	W	2-1	
19 v West Bromwich Albion a	W	1-0	1
20 v Derby County h	D	0-0	
21 v Derby County a	W	1-0	
22 v Watford (Villa Park)	L	0-1	

Total: 10 appearances, 3 goals.

Milk Cup:

25 v Swindon Town a	L	0-1	
26 v Swindon Town h	W	4-1	1
27 v Arsenal h	D	1-1	
28 v Arsenal a	L	0-1	

Total: 4 appearances, 1 goal.

Associate Members Cup:

9 v Torquay United h	W	5-1	2
10 v Brentford h	W	2-0	2
11 v Millwall h	L	0-1	

Total: 3 appearances, 4 goals.

1984/85 PLYMOUTH ARGYLE
Football League:

325 v Burnley a	D	1-1	
326 v Reading h	L	1-2	
327 v Lincoln City a	D	2-2	1
328 v AFC Bournemouth h	D	0-0	
329 v York City h	D	1-1	
330 v Bolton Wanderers a	L	2-7	1
331 v Preston North End h	W	6-4	1
332 v Gillingham a	D	3-3	1
333 v Hull City h	L	0-1	
334 v Derby County a	L	1-3	1

335 v Rotherham United h	W	1-0	
336 v Orient a	L	0-3	
337 v Doncaster Rovers a	L	3-4	2
338 v Bristol Rovers h	W	3-2	1
339 v Bradford City h	D	0-0	
340 v Wigan Athletic a	L	0-1	
341 v Walsall h	L	1-3	1
342 v Swansea City a	W	2-0	1
343 v Cambridge United h	W	2-0	1
344 v Millwall h	W	3-1	1
345 v Bristol City a	L	3-4	3
346 v Newport County a	L	0-1	
347 v Brentford h	D	1-1	1
348 v Preston North End a	W	2-1	
349 v Bolton Wanderers h	W	2-0	1
350 v York City a	D	0-0	
351 v Bristol Rovers a	L	0-1	
352 v Doncaster Rovers h	W	2-1	1
353 v Orient h	D	1-1	
354 v Rotherham United a	W	2-0	1
355 v Derby County h	L	0-1	
356 v Gillingham h	D	1-1	1(p)
357 v Hull City a	D	2-2	2
358 v Burnley h	D	2-2	2(1p)
359 v Bradford City a	L	0-1	
360 v Bristol City h	W	1-0	
361 v Brentford a	L	1-3	1(p)
362 v Wigan Athletic h	W	1-0	1
363 v Lincoln City h	W	2-0	2
364 v Walsall a	W	3-0	1
365 v Reading a	D	1-1	
366 v Swansea City h	L	1-2	1
367 v Cambridge United a	D	1-1	1(p)
368 v Newport County h	W	1-0	
369 v Millwall a	L	0-2	

Total: 45 appearances, 31 goals (4 penalties).

<u>FA Cup:</u>

23 v Barnet h	W	3-0	1
24 v Hereford United h	D	0-0	
25 v Hereford United a	L	0-2	

Total: 3 appearances, 1 goal.

<u>Milk Cup:</u>

29 v Torquay United h	W	1-0
30 v Torquay United a	W	1-0
31 v Birmingham City a	L	1-4
32 v Birmingham City h	W	1-0

Total: 4 appearances.

<u>Freight Rover Trophy:</u>

12 v AFC Bournemouth a	L	0-2

Total: 1 appearance.

1985/86 ROTHERHAM UNITED

<u>Football League:</u>

370 v Bolton Wanderers a	D	1-1	
371 v Lincoln City h	W	1-0	
372 v Chesterfield a	L	0-2	
373 v Bristol City h	W	2-0	1(p)
374 v Swansea City a	L	0-1	
375 v Reading h	L	1-2	
376 v Walsall a	L	1-3	
377 v Doncaster Rovers h	W	2-1	
378 v Brentford a	D	1-1	
379 v Cardiff City h	W	3-0	
380 v Wolverhampton Wanderers h	L	1-2	1
381 v Bristol Rovers a	L	2-5	1
382 v Plymouth Argyle h	D	1-1	1
383 v Newport County a	D	0-0	
384 v York City a	L	1-2	
385 v Gillingham h	D	1-1	
386 v Wigan Athletic a	L	0-2	
387 v Bury h	W	2-0	1
388 v Notts County h	W	1-0	
389 v AFC Bournemouth a	W	2-1	1
390 v Lincoln City a	D	0-0	
391 v Darlington a	D	2-2	
392 v Chesterfield h	L	1-2	
393 v Blackpool h	W	4-1	
394 v Bristol City a	L	1-3	1
395 v Bolton Wanderers h	W	4-0	2
396 v Swansea City h	W	4-1	3
397 v Newport County h	D	0-0	
398 v Walsall h	W	3-0	1
399 v Brentford h	L	1-2	

Total: 30 appearances, 13 goals (1 penalty).

<u>FA Cup:</u>

26 v Wolverhampton Wanderers h	W	6-0	1
27 v Burnley h	W	4-1	1
28 v Frickley Athletic a	W	3-1	1
29 v Arsenal a	L	1-5	1

Total: 4 appearances, 4 goals.

<u>Milk Cup:</u>

33 v Sheffield United h	L	1-3
34 v Sheffield United a	L	1-5

Total: 2 appearances.

Freight Rover Trophy:

13 v York City a	D	0-0	
14 v Hartlepool United h	W	3-0	
15 v Wigan Athletic a	L	0-3	

Total: 3 appearances.

1985/86 PLYMOUTH ARGYLE (loan)

Football League:

400 v AFC Bournemouth a	W	3-1	
401 v Rotherham United h	W	4-0	2
402 v Bury h	W	3-0	2
403 v Lincoln City a	D	1-1	1
404 v Wigan Athletic a	L	0-3	
405 v Bolton Wanderers h	W	4-1	1
406 v Blackpool h	W	3-1	1
407 v Bristol City h	W	4-0	2
408 v Darlington a	W	2-0	1

Total: 9 appearances, 10 goals.

1986/87 ROTHERHAM UNITED

Football League:

409 v Fulham h	D	0-0	
410 v Port Vale a	D	1-1	

Total: 2 appearances.

Littlewoods Cup:

35 v Doncaster Rovers a	D	1-1	1
36 v Doncaster Rovers h	W	4-1	1

Total: 2 appearances, 2 goals.

1986/87 PLYMOUTH ARGYLE

Football League:

411 v Hull City a	W	3-0	
412 v Brighton & Hove Albion h	D	2-2	
413 v Barnsley a	D	1-1	
414 v Blackburn Rovers a	W	2-1	
415 v Leeds United h	D	1-1	
416 v Grimsby Town a	D	1-1	
417 v Sheffield United h	W	1-0	1
418 v Sunderland h	L	2-4	1
419 v Ipswich Town h	W	2-0	
420 v Millwall a	L	1-3	
421 v Crystal Palace h	W	3-1	2
422 v Shrewsbury Town a	D	1-1	
423 v West Bromwich Albion h	W	1-0	
424 v Huddersfield Town a	W	2-1	1
425 v Oldham Athletic h	W	3-2	1
426 v Stoke City a	L	0-1	
427 v Derby County h	D	1-1	1
428 v Ipswich Town a	L	0-3	
429 v Portsmouth h	L	2-3	
430 v West Bromwich Albion a	D	0-0	
431 v Birmingham City a	L	2-3	1
432 v Hull City h	W	4-0	2
433 v Bradford City h	W	3-2	1
434 v Reading a	L	0-2	
435 v Blackburn Rovers h	D	1-1	
436 v Sheffield United a	L	1-2	
437 v Barnsley h	W	2-0	
438 v Millwall h	W	1-0	1
439 v Sunderland a	L	1-2	1
440 v Grimsby Town h	W	5-0	2
441 v Leeds United a	L	0-4	
442 v Shrewsbury Town h	W	3-2	2
443 v Brighton & Hove Albion a	D	1-1	1
444 v Crystal Palace a	D	0-0	
445 v Birmingham City h	D	0-0	
446 v Portsmouth a	W	1-0	
447 v Huddersfield Town h	D	1-1	
448 v Oldham Athletic a	L	1-2	
449 v Stoke City h	L	1-3	
450 v Derby County a	L	2-4	

Total: 40 appearances, 18 goals.

FA Cup:

30 v Bristol City a	D	1-1	
31 v Bristol City h	W	3-1	1
32 v Arsenal a	L	1-6	

Total: 3 appearances, 1 goal.

Full Members Cup:

1 v Ipswich Town a	L	2-3	1

Total: 1 appearance, 1 goal.

1987/88 PLYMOUTH ARGYLE

Football League:

451 v Manchester City a	L	1-2	
452 v Ipswich Town h	D	0-0	
453 v Huddersfield Town h	W	6-1	2
454 v Reading a	W	1-0	
455 v Sheffield United h	W	1-0	
456 v Barnsley a	L	1-2	1
457 v West Bromwich Albion h	D	3-3	2
458 v Bradford City a	L	1-3	
459 v Leicester City a	L	0-4	
460 v Birmingham City h	D	1-1	1
461 v AFC Bournemouth a	D	2-2	
462 v Stoke City a	L	0-1	
463 v Leeds United h	W	6-3	1
464 v Millwall h	L	1-2	
465 v Blackburn Rovers a	D	1-1	
466 v Hull City h	W	3-1	1(p)
467 v Crystal Palace a	L	1-5	
468 v Swindon Town a	D	1-1	

468 v Swindon Town a	D	1-1	
469 v Middlesbrough h	L	0-1	
470 v Oldham Athletic a	W	1-0	1
471 v Shrewsbury Town h	W	2-0	
472 v Huddersfield Town a	L	1-2	
473 v Bradford City h	W	2-1	
474 v Birmingham City a	W	1-0	1(p)
475 v Leicester City h	W	4-0	2
476 v Reading h	L	1-3	1(p)
477 v West Bromwich Albion a	L	0-1	
478 v Manchester City h	W	3-2	1
479 v Ipswich Town a	W	2-1	
480 v Aston Villa a	L	2-5	1
481 v Leeds United a	L	0-1	
482 v Stoke City h	W	3-0	2
483 v Hull City a	D	1-1	
484 v Blackburn Rovers h	W	3-0	
485 v Swindon Town h	W	1-0	
486 v Millwall a	L	2-3	
487 v Barnsley h	D	0-0	
488 v Sheffield United a	L	0-1	
489 v Crystal Palace h	L	1-3	
490 v AFC Bournemouth h	L	1-2	
491 v Middlesbrough a	L	1-3	
492 v Oldham Athletic h	W	1-0	
493 v Shrewsbury Town a	L	1-2	

Total: 43 appearances, 17 goals (3 penalties).

<u>FA Cup:</u>

33 v Colchester United h	W	2-0	
34 v Shrewsbury Town h	W	1-0	
35 v Manchester City a	L	1-3	1

Total: 3 appearances, 1 goal.

<u>Littlewoods Cup:</u>

37 v Peterborough United a	L	1-4	1

Total: 1 appearance, 1 goal.

<u>Simod Cup:</u>

2 v Manchester City a	L	2-6	1

Total: 1 appearance, 1 goal.

1988/89 PLYMOUTH ARGYLE

<u>Football League:</u>

494 v Walsall a	D	2-2	1
495 v Hull City h	W	2-0	1
496 v Watford a	L	0-3	
497 v Stoke City h	W	4-0	3
498 v Leicester City a	L	0-1	
499 v West Bromwich Albion h	D	1-1	1
500 v Crystal Palace a	L	1-4	
501 v Birmingham City a	W	1-0	1
502 v Bradford City h	W	3-1	2
503 v Manchester City h	L	0-1	
504 v Chelsea a	L	0-5	
505 v Shrewsbury Town h	D	0-0	
506 v Barnsley a	L	1-3	
507 v Blackburn Rovers h	W	4-3	4
508 v Portsmouth a	L	0-2	
598 v Oxford United a	W	1-0	1
510 v Oldham Athletic h	W	3-0	1
511 v Ipswich Town a	D	2-2	
512 v Brighton & Hove Albion h	W	3-0	2(1p)
513 v AFC Bournemouth h	D	1-1	
514 v Sunderland h	L	1-4	1(p)
515 v Swindon Town a	L	0-1	
516 v Leeds United a	L	0-2	
517 v Watford h	W	1-0	
518 v Brighton & Hove Albion a	D	2-2	1
519 v Walsall h	W	2-0	1
520 v Birmingham City h	L	0-1	
521 v Bradford City a	D	1-1	
522 v Chelsea h	L	0-1	
523 v Manchester City a	L	0-2	
524 v Shrewsbury Town a	L	0-2	
525 v Portsmouth h	L	0-1	
526 v Blackburn Rovers a	W	2-1	1
527 v Leicester City h	D	1-1	
528 v Hull City a	L	0-3	
529 v Swindon Town h	W	4-1	1(p)
530 v Stoke City a	D	2-2	1(p)
531 v Sunderland a	L	1-2	1
532 v Leeds United h	W	1-0	
533 v West Bromwich Albion a	D	2-2	
534 v Crystal Palace h	L	0-2	
535 v Barnsley h	L	1-2	
536 v Oldham Athletic a	D	2-2	
537 v Ipswich Town h	L	0-1	
538 v Oxford United h	W	3-1	
539 v AFC Bournemouth a	D	0-0	

Total: 46 appearances, 24 goals (4 penalties).

<u>FA Cup:</u>

36 v Cambridge United h	W	2-0	1
37 v Everton h	D	1-1	
38 v Everton a	L	0-4	

Total: 3 appearances, 1 goal.

<u>Littlewoods Cup:</u>

38 v Hereford United a	W	3-0	
39 v Hereford United h	W	3-2	
40 v Manchester City a	L	0-1	
41 v Manchester City h	L	3-6	1

Total: 4 appearances, 1 goal.

Simod Cup:

3 v Chelsea a	L	2-6	

Total: 1 appearance.

1989/90 PLYMOUTH ARGYLE

Football League:

540 v Oxford United h	W	2-0	
541 v West Ham United a	L	2-3	
542 v Barnsley h	W	2-1	
543 v Oldham Athletic a	L	2-3	
544 v Portsmouth a	W	3-0	2(1p)
545 v Sheffield United h	D	0-0	
546 v Wolverhampton Wanderers a	L	0-1	
547 v Swindon Town a	L	0-3	
548 v Brighton & Hove Albion h	W	2-1	1
549 v Stoke City h	W	3-0	1(p)
550 v Middlesbrough a	W	2-0	
551 v Leicester City h	W	3-1	
552 v Ipswich Town a	L	0-3	
553 v Blackburn Rovers h	D	2-2	
554 v Leeds United a	L	1-2	
555 v Bradford City h	D	1-1	1
556 v Watford a	W	2-1	1
557 v Sunderland a	L	1-3	
558 v Port Vale h	L	1-2	1
559 v Oxford United a	L	2-3	1(p)
560 v Portsmouth h	L	0-2	
561 v West Bromwich Albion h	D	2-2	
562 v AFC Bournemouth a	D	2-2	1(p)
563 v West Ham United h	D	1-1	1
564 v Barnsley a	D	1-1	
565 v Wolverhampton Wanderers h	L	0-1	
566 v Sheffield United a	L	0-1	
567 v Port Vale a	L	0-3	
568 v Sunderland h	W	3-0	2
569 v Brighton & Hove Albion a	L	1-2	
570 v Swindon Town h	L	0-3	
571 v Stoke City a	D	0-0	
572 v Middlesbrough h	L	1-2	
573 v Leicester City	D	1-1	
574 v Ipswich Town h	W	1-0	
575 v Newcastle United a	L	1-3	
576 v Blackburn Rovers a	L	0-2	
577 v Leeds United h	D	1-1	1(p)
578 v AFC Bournemouth h	W	1-0	1(p)
579 v West Bromwich Albion a	W	3-0	
580 v Oldham Athletic h	W	2-0	
581 v Newcastle United h	D	1-1	1
582 v Hull City a	D	3-3	
583 v Watford h	D	0-0	

Total: 44 games, 15 goals (6 penalties).

FA Cup:

39 v Oxford h	L	0-1	

Total: 1 appearance.

Littlewoods Cup:

42 v Cardiff City a	W	3-0	2(1p)
43 v Cardiff City h	L	0-2	
44 v Arsenal a	L	0-2	
45 v Arsenal h	L	1-6	1

Total: 4 appearances, 3 goals (1 penalty).

Zenith Data Systems Cup:

4 v West Ham United a	L	2-5	

Total: 1 appearance.

The figure on the left denotes number of match played in competition referred to. The Football League Group Cup, the Football League Trophy, the Associate Members Cup and the Freight Rover competitions run consecutively since, in essence, they are the same competition, i.e. competitions for Associate Members of the Football League. The same principle applies to the Full Members Cup, the Simod Cup and the Zenith Data Systems Cup. Appearance figures include those made as substitute.

CLUB-BY-CLUB APPEARANCES

CLUB	FL	FA	LC	EW	WC	FG	FT	AM	FR	FM	SC	ZC	TOT
LIVERPOOL	-	-	-	-	-	-	-	-	-	-	-	-	-
SWANSEA *	6	-	-	-	-	-	-	-	-	-	-	-	6
SHEFF WED	91	4	12	-	-	-	-	-	-	-	-	-	107
LINCOLN	9	-	-	-	-	-	-	-	-	-	-	-	9
NEWPORT	183	8	12	5	13	4	4	-	-	-	-	-	229
PLYMOUTH	80	13	8	-	-	-	-	3	1	-	-	-	105
ROTHERHAM	30	4	2	-	-	-	-	-	3	-	-	-	39
PLYMOUTH *	9	-	-	-	-	-	-	-	-	-	-	-	9
ROTHERHAM	2	-	2	-	-	-	-	-	-	-	-	-	4
PLYMOUTH	173	10	9	-	-	-	-	-	-	1	2	1	196
TOTALS	583	39	45	5	13	4	4	3	4	1	2	1	704

CLUB-BY-CLUB GOALS

CLUB	FL	FA	FL	EW	WC	FG	FT	AM	FR	FM	SC	ZC	TOT
LIVERPOOL	-	-	-	-	-	-	-	-	-	-	-	-	-
SWANSEA *	2	-	-	-	-	-	-	-	-	-	-	-	2
SHEFF WED	31	1	5	-	-	-	-	-	-	-	-	-	37
LINCOLN	1	-	-	-	-	-	-	-	-	-	-	-	1
NEWPORT	66	4	5	4	5	-	2	-	-	-	-	-	86
PLYMOUTH	43	4	1	-	-	-	-	4	-	-	-	-	52
ROTHERHAM	13	4	-	-	-	-	-	-	-	-	-	-	17
PLYMOUTH *	10	-	-	-	-	-	-	-	-	-	-	-	10
ROTHERHAM	-	-	2	-	-	-	-	-	-	-	-	-	2
PLYMOUTH	74	3	5	-	-	-	-	-	-	1	1	-	84
TOTALS	240	16	18	4	5	-	2	4	-	1	1	-	291

SEASON-BY-SEASON APPEARANCES

	FL	FA	LC	EW	FG	FT	AM	FR	FM	SC	ZC	TOT
1975/76 SWANSEA *	6	-	-	-	-	-	-	-	-	-	-	6
1976/77 SHEFF W	39	2	2	-	-	-	-	-	-	-	-	43
1977/78 SHEFF W	44	2	6	-	-	-	-	-	-	-	-	52
1978/79 SHEFF W	8	-	4	-	-	-	-	-	-	-	-	12
1978/79 LINCOLN	9	-	-	-	-	-	-	-	-	-	-	9
1978/79 NEWPORT	20	-	-	-	-	-	-	-	-	-	-	20
1979/80 NEWPORT	34	1	2	-	-	-	-	-	-	-	-	37
1980/81 NEWPORT	45	1	4	5	-	-	-	-	-	-	-	55
1981/82 NEWPORT	38	1	2	-	4	-	-	-	-	-	-	45
1982/83 NEWPORT	46	5	4	-	-	4	-	-	-	-	-	59
1983/84 PLYMOUTH	35	10	4	-	-	-	3	-	-	-	-	52
1984/85 PLYMOUTH	45	3	4	-	-	-	-	1	-	-	-	53
1985/86 ROTH'M	30	4	2	-	-	-	-	3	-	-	-	39
1985/86 PLYMOUTH *	9	-	-	-	-	-	-	-	-	-	-	9
1986/87 ROTH'M	2	-	2	-	-	-	-	-	-	-	-	4

1986/87 PLYMOUTH	4	0	3	-	-	-	-	-	-	1	-	44
1987/88 PLYMOUTH	43	3	1	-	-	-	-	-	-	1	-	48
1988/89 PLYMOUTH	46	3	4	-	-	-	-	-	-	1	-	54
1989/90 PLYMOUTH	44	1	4	-	-	-	-	-	-	-	1	50
TOTALS:	583	39	45	5	4	4	3	4	1	2	1	691

SEASON-BY-SEASON GOALS

	FL	FA	LC	EW	FG	FT	AM	FR	FM	SC	ZC	TOT
1975/76 SWANSEA *	2	-	-	-	-	-	-	-	-	-	-	2
1976/77 SHEFF W	14	1	-	-	-	-	-	-	-	-	-	15
1977/78 SHEFF W	16	-	5	-	-	-	-	-	-	-	-	21
1978/79 SHEFF W	1	-	-	-	-	-	-	-	-	-	-	1
1978/79 LINCOLN	1	-	-	-	-	-	-	-	-	-	-	1
1978/79 NEWPORT	7	-	-	-	-	-	-	-	-	-	-	7
1979/80 NEWPORT	8	-	1	-	-	-	-	-	-	-	-	9
1980/81 NEWPORT	13	-	2	4	-	-	-	-	-	-	-	19
1981/82 NEWPORT	13	-	-	-	-	-	-	-	-	-	-	13
1982/83 NEWPORT	25	4	2	-	-	2	-	-	-	-	-	33
1983/84 PLYMOUTH	12	3	1	-	-	-	4	-	-	-	-	20
1984/85 PLYMOUTH	31	1	-	-	-	-	-	-	-	-	-	32
1985/86 ROTH'M	13	4	-	-	-	-	-	-	-	-	-	17
1985/86 PLYMOUTH *	10	-	-	-	-	-	-	-	-	-	-	10
1986/87 ROTH'M	-	-	2	-	-	-	-	-	-	-	-	2
1986/87 PLYMOUTH	18	1	-	-	-	-	-	-	1	-	-	20
1987/88 PLYMOUTH	17	1	1	-	-	-	-	-	-	1	-	20
1988/89 PLYMOUTH	24	1	1	-	-	-	-	-	-	-	-	26
1989/90 PLYMOUTH	15	-	3	-	-	-	-	-	-	-	-	18
TOTALS:	240	16	18	4	-	2	4	-	1	1	-	286
									(+ Welsh Cup)			5
												291

Key: FL = Football League; FA = FA Cup; LC = League Cup; EW = European Cup-Winners Cup; WC = Welsh Cup; FG = Football League Group Cup; FT = Football League Trophy; AM = Associate Members Cup; FR = Freight Rover Trophy; FM = Full Members Cup; SC = Simod Cup; ZC = Zenith Data Systems Cup; * = on loan. Appearance totals include those made as substitute.

SUMMARY:APPEARANCES (GOALS)

	LEAGUE	OTHER	TOTAL
CAREER:	583 (240)	121 (51)	704 (291)
PLYMOUTH:	262 (127)	48 (19)	310 (146)
NEWPORT:	183 (66)	46 (20)	229 (86)
SHEFF WEDS:	91 (31)	16 (6)	107 (37)
ROTHERHAM:	32 (13)	11 (6)	43 (19)
LINCOLN:	9 (1)	- (-)	9 (1)
SWANSEA:	6 (2)	- (-)	6 (2)

OPPONENTS CLUB-BY-CLUB:

FOR SWANSEA:
1 v Barnsley, Bradford City, Darlington, Doncaster Rovers, Reading, Torquay United.
Total: 6.

FOR SHEFFIELD WEDNESDAY:
7 v Bury;
5 v Doncaster Rovers, Gillingham, Lincoln City, Peterborough United;
4 v Chester, Chesterfield, Oxford United, Rotherham United, Shrewsbury Town, Swindon Town, Tranmere Rovers, Wrexham;
3 v Port Vale, Portsmouth, Preston North End, Walsall;
2 v Blackpool, Bradford City, Brighton & Hove Albion, Cambridge United, Carlisle United, Colchester United, Crystal Palace, Exeter City, Hereford United, Mansfield Town, Plymouth Argyle, Reading, York City.
1 v Aston Villa, Darlington, Everton, Grimsby Town, Millwall, Northampton, Southend United, Stockport County, Watford, Wigan Athletic.
Total: 107.

FOR LINCOLN CITY:
1 v Chesterfield, Colchester United, Gillingham, Mansfield Town, Oxford United, Peterborough United, Plymouth Argyle, Sheffield Wednesday, Swindon Town.
Total: 9

FOR NEWPORT COUNTY:
10 v Plymouth Argyle;
9 v Exeter City, Portsmouth;
8 v Huddersfield Town, Walsall;
7 v Doncaster Rovers;
6 v AFC Bournemouth, Brentford, Gilingham, Lincoln City.
5 v Chesterfield, Millwall, Oxford United, Reading, Torquay United.
4 v Bradford City, Burnley, Chester, Everton, Halifax Town, Hereford United, Preston North End, Sheffield United, Southend United, Swindon Town, Wigan Athletic.
3 v Barnsley, Bristol City, Bristol Rovers, Carlisle United, Colchester United, Fulham, Northampton Town, Orient, Port Vale, Rochdale, Wimbledon, York City.
2 v Aldershot, Cardiff City, Carl Zeiss Jena, Charlton Athletic, Crewe Alexandra, Crusaders, Darlington, Enfield, Grimsby Town, Hull City, Notts County, Peterborough United, Rotherham United, Scunthorpe United, Stockport County, Wrexham.
1 v Blackpool, Hartlepool United, Haugar, Oldham Athletic.
13 v Welsh Cup opponents.
Total: 229.

FOR PLYMOUTH ARGYLE:
11 v AFC Bournemouth, Hull City;
9 v Bradford City, Ipswich Town, Millwall, West Bromwich Albion;
8 v Barnsley, Birmingham City, Blackburn Rovers, Leeds United, Manchester City, Oldham Athletic, Sheffield United, Swindon Town;
7 v Oxford United, Shrewsbury Town, Stoke City;
6 v Brighton & Hove Albion, Crystal Palace, Derby County, Leicester City Portsmouth, Sunderland;
5 v Arsenal, Brentford, Bristol City, Bolton Wanderers, Lincoln City, Newport County, Reading, Rotherham United, Walsall, Watford, Wigan Athletic;

4 v Bristol Rovers, Hereford United, Huddersfield Town, Middlesbrough, Port Vale;
3 v Burnley, Cambridge United, Chelsea, Gillingham, Preston North End, Southend United, Torquay United, West Ham United;
2 v Cardiff City, Darlington, Doncaster Rovers, Everton, Grimsby Town, Newcastle United, Orient, Scunthorpe United, Swansea City, Wolverhampton Wanderers, York City;
1 v Aston Villa, Barking, Barnet, Blackpool, Bury, Colchester United, Exeter City, Peterborough United, Wimbledon.
Total: 310

ROTHERHAM UNITED:
3 v Doncaster Rovers;
2 v Bolton Wanderers, Brentford, Bristol City, Chesterfield, Lincoln City, Newport County, Sheffield United, Swansea City, Walsall, Wigan Athletic, Wolverhampton Wanderers, York City.
1 v AFC Bournemouth, Arsenal, Blackpool, Bristol Rovers, Burnley, Bury, Cardiff City, Darlington, Frickley Athletic, Fulham, Gillingham, Hartlepool United, Notts County, Plymouth Argyle, Port Vale, Reading.
Total: 43.

OPPPONENTS (CAREER)

18v AFC Bournemouth, Doncaster Rovers, Lincoln City, Portsmouth, Walsall;
17v Oxford United, Swindon Town;
16v Bradford City, Gillingham;
15v Millwall;
14v Reading, Sheffield United;
13v Brentford, Hull City, Plymouth Argyle, various Welsh Cup opponents;
12v Barnsley, Chesterfield, Exeter City, Huddersfield Town, Wigan Athletic;
11v Port Vale, Rotherham United, Shrewsbury Town;
10v Bristol City, Hereford United, Preston North End;
9 v Blackburn Rovers, Bury, Ipswich Town, Oldham Athletic, Peterborough United, Torquay United, West Bromwich Albion, York City;
8 v Birmingham City, Brighton & Hove Albion, Bristol Rovers, Burnley, Chester, Crystal Palace, Leeds United, Manchester City, Southend United, Stoke City;
7 v Bolton Wanderers, Colchester United, Darlington, Everton, Newport County;
6 v Arsenal, Derby County, Leicester City, Sunderland, Watford, Wrexham;
5 v Blackpool, Cambridge United, Cardiff City, Carlisle United, Grimsby Town, Orient;
4 v Fulham, Halifax Town, Middlesbrough, Northampton Town, Scunthorpe United, Swansea City, Tranmere Rovers, Wimbledon, Wolverhampton Wanderers;
3 v Chelsea, Mansfield Town, Notts County; Rochdale, Stockport County, West Ham United;
2 v Aldershot, Aston Villa, Carl Zeiss Jena, Charlton Athletic, Crewe Alexandra, Crusaders, Enfield, Hartlepool United, Newcastle United;
1 v Barking, Barnet, Frickley Athletic, Hagaur, Sheffield Wednesday.
Total: 704.

GOALS OPPONENTS-BY-OPPONENTS

FOR SWANSEA
1 v Bradford City, Doncaster Rovers.
Total: 2

FOR SHEFFIELD WEDNESDAY
3 v Bury, Chesterfield, Portsmouth;
2 v Blackpool, Bradford City, Chester, Oxford United, Peterborough United, Preston North End, Swindon Town, Tranmere Rovers, Walsall, Wrexham, York City;
1 v Carlisle United, Doncaster Rovers, Everton, Lincoln City, Port Vale, Stockport County.
Total: 37

FOR LINCOLN CITY
1 v Oxford United.
Total: 1.

FOR NEWPORT COUNTY
5 v Chesterfield, Lincoln City, Plymouth Argyle, various Welsh Cup goals ;
4 v Bristol Rovers, Exeter City;
3 v Orient, Oxford United, Enfield, Southend United, Walsall, Wrexham;
2 v Bradford City, Carlisle United, Carl Zeiss Jena, Doncaster Rovers, Haugar, Hereford United, Millwall, Portsmouth, Preston North End, Reading, Sheffield United, Wigan Athletic;
1 v Aldershot, AFC Bournemouth, Brentford, Bristol City, Burnley, Charlton Athletic, Crewe Alexandra, Everton, Fulham, Gillingham, Northampton Town, Port Vale, Swindon Town, Wimbledon, York City.
Total: 86.

FOR PLYMOUTH ARGYLE
8 v Hull City;
7 v Stoke City;
6 v Bristol City, Sunderland;
5 v Brentford, Brighton & Hove Albion, Blackburn Rovers, Lincoln City;
4 v Birmingham City, Bolton Wanderers, Bradford City, Manchester City, Rotherham United, Walsall, West Bromwich Albion;
3 v Cambridge United, Doncaster Rovers, Oldham Athletic, Port Vale;
2 v AFC Bournemouth, Burnley, Bury, Cardiff City, Crystal Palace, Derby County, Gillingham, Grimsby Town, Huddersfield Town, Leeds United, Leicester City, Millwall, Oxford United, Portsmouth, Shrewsbury Town, Southend United, Swansea City, Swindon Town, Torquay United, Wigan Athletic;
1 v Arsenal, Aston Villa, Barnet, Barnsley, Blackpool, Bristol Rovers, Darlington, Huddersfield Town, Ipswich Town, Newcastle United, Newport County, Peterborough United, Preston North End, Reading, Sheffield United, Walsall, Watford, West Ham United, Wimbledon.
Total: 146.

FOR ROTHERHAM
3 v Swansea City;
2 v Bristol City, Bolton Wanderers, Doncaster Rovers, Wolverhampton Wanderers;
1 v AFC Bournemouth, Arsenal, Bristol Rovers, Burnley, Bury, Frickley Athletic, Plymouth Argyle, Walsall.
Total: 17.

GOALS (CAREER)

11 v Lincoln City, Walsall;
10 v Doncaster Rovers;
9 v Bradford City, Bristol City;
8 v Chesterfield, Hull City, Oxford United;
7 v Portsmouth, Stoke City;
6 v Brentford, Bristol Rovers, Bury, Bolton Wanderers, Plymouth Argyle, Sunderland;
5 v Blackburn Rovers, Brighton & Hove Albion, Port Vale, Preston North End, Southend United, Swansea City, Swindon Town, Wrexham, various Welsh Cup opponents;
4 v AFC Bournemouth, Birmingham City, Burnley, Exeter City, Manchester City, Millwall, Peterborough United, Rotherham United, West Bromwich Albion, Wigan Athletic;
3 v Blackpool, Cambridge United, Carlisle United, Enfield, Gillingham, Huddersfield Town, Oldham Athletic, Orient, Reading, Sheffield United, York City;
2 v Arsenal, Cardiff City, Carl Zeiss Jena, Chester, Crystal Palace, Derby County, Everton, Grimsby Town, Haugar, Hereford United, Leeds United, Leicester City, Shrewsbury Town, Torquay United, Tranmere Rovers, Wimbledon, Wolverhampton Wanderers;
1 v Aldershot, Barnet, Barnsley, Charlton Athletic, Crewe Alexandra, Darlington, Frickley Athletic, Fulham, Ipswich Town, Newcastle United, Newport County, Northampton Town, Stockport County, Watford, West Ham United.
Total: 291.

SIGNIFICANT MILESTONES

Oct 18, 1975 Football League debut, Doncaster Rovers v SWANSEA CITY a. L 1-2 (scored).
Sep 11, 1976 Sheffield Wednesday debut, v Swindon Town a. L 2-5 (scored).
Sep 20, 1976 Football League Cup debut, SHEFFIELD WEDNESDAY v Watford h, third round. W 3-1.
Nov 20, 1976 FA Cup debut, SHEFFIELD WEDNESDAY v Stockport County h, first round. W 2-0 (scored).
Oct 13, 1978 Lincoln City debut, v Colchester United h. D 0-0.
Oct 21, 1978 100th Football League appearance, LINCOLN CITY v Swindon Town h. L 0-3.
Feb 24, 1979 Newport County debut, v Huddersfield a. W 1-0.
Sep 16, 1980 European Cup-Winners Cup debut, NEWPORT COUNTY v Crusaders h. W 4-0.
Aug 19, 1980 50th Football League goal, NEWPORT COUNTY v Charlton Athletic h. L 1-2.
Apr 18, 1981 200th Football League appearance, NEWPORT COUNTY v Exeter City h. W 2-1 (scored).
Aug 15, 1981 Football League Group Cup debut, NEWPORT COUNTY v Torquay United h, group match. D 0-0.
Aug 14, 1982 Football League Trophy debut, NEWPORT COUNTY v Torquay United h, group match. L 0-1.
NOV 6, 1982 50th Football League goal for Newport, v Reading a. L 2-4.
Nov 23, 1982 First senior hat-trick, NEWPORT COUNTY v Enfield h, FA Cup first round replay.
Apr 30, 1983 First Football League hat-trick, NEWPORT COUNTY v Wrexham h + 100th Football League goal (third).
Aug 27, 1983 Plymouth Argyle debut, v Wigan Athletic h. D 0-0.
Oct 18, 1983 300th Football League appearance, PLYMOUTH ARGYLE v Bristol Rovers h. D 1-1.
Aug 17, 1985 Rotherham United debut, v Bolton Wanderers a. D 1-1.
Jan 11, 1986 150th Football League goal, Bristol City v ROTHERHAM UNITED A. L 1-3.
Apr 5, 1986 400th Football League appearance, AFC Bournemouth v PLYMOUTH ARGYLE a. W 3-1.
Apr 26, 1986 50th Football League goal for Plymouth Argyle, v Blackpool h. W 3-1.
Sep 6, 1986 Plymouth Argyle second debut, v Hull City a. W 3-1.
Sep 16, 1986 Full Members Cup debut, Ipswich Town v PLYMOUTH ARGYLE a, first round. L 2-3 (scored).

Nov 10, 1987 Simod Cup debut, Manchester City v PLYMOUTH ARGYLE a, first round. L 2-6 (scored).
Mar 12, 1988 200th Football League goal, PLYMOUTH ARGYLE v Stoke City h. W 3-0.
Oct 1, 1988 500th Football League appearance, Crystal Palace v PLYMOUTH ARGYLE a. L 1-4.
Nov 5, 1988 100th Football League goal for Plymouth Argyle, v Blackburn Rovers h. W 4-3.
Nov 29, 1989 Zenith Data Systems Cup debut, West Ham United v PLYMOUTH ARGYLE a. L 2-5.
Mar 17, 1990 250th Football League game for Plymouth Argyle, v Stoke City a. D 0-0.
Mar 24, 1990 300th Football League game for Plymouth Argyle, v Leicester City a. D 1-1.
Apr 16, 1990 700th senior professional appearance, West Bromwich Albion v PLYMOUTH ARGYLE a. W 3-0.

PLYMOUTH ARGYLE PLAYERS, CONSECUTIVE APPEARANCES, FOOTBALL LEAGUE

1 PAT JONES	AUG 23, 1947 - OCT 31, 1954	276
2 JOHNNY WILLIAMS	DEC 20, 1958 - MAR 9, 1963	179
3 FRED CRAIG	AUG 25, 1923 - SEP 22, 1926	174
4 GORDON NISBET	FEB 4, 1983 - MAR 28, 1987	165
5 KEVIN HODGES	NOV 12, 1980 - MAR 20, 1984	150
6 GEOFF CRUDGINGTON	OCT 6, 1980 - SEP 22, 1984	148
7 JOHN HORE	NOV 21, 1969 - APR 1, 1972	112
8 JOHN SIMS	SEP 17, 1980 - NOV 27, 1982	102
9 TOMMY TYNAN	OCT 10, 1987 - DEC 26, 1989	100
10 COLIN SULLIVAN	NOV 27, 1971 - NOV 10, 1973	90

PLYMOUTH ARGYLE PLAYERS, CONSECUTIVE APPEARANCES, ALL MATCHES

1 JOHNNY WILLIAMS	DEC 20, 1958 - MAR 9, 1963	198
2 PAT JONES	JAN 10, 1950 - OCT 31, 1954	185
3 FRED CRAIG	AUG 25, 1923 - SEP 22, 1926	181
4 KEVIN HODGES	NOV 12, 1980 - MAR 20, 1984	179
5 GEOFF CRUDGINGTON	OCT 6, 1979 - SEP 22, 1984	165
6 JOHN HORE	NOV 21, 1969 - APR 1, 1972	119
7 TOMMY TYNAN	OCT 10, 1987 - DEC 26, 1989	115
8 JOHN SIMS	SEP 17, 1980 - NOV 27, 1982	114
9 PAT JONES	AUG 23, 1947 - JAN 7, 1950	112
10 COLIN SULLIVAN	NOV 27, 1971 - NOV 10, 1973	99

LEAGUE APPEARANCES, PLYMOUTH ARGYLE PLAYERS

1 SAMMY BLACK (1924-38)	470
2 KEVIN HODGES (1978-)	470
3 PAT JONES (1946-58)	425
4 JOHNNY WILLIAMS (1955-66)	411
5 JOHN HORE (1964-76)	400
6 JACK LESLIE (1921-35)	383
7 FRED CRAIG (1920-30)	361
8 GEORGE ROBERTSON (1950-64)	359
9 BILL SHORTT (1946-56)	342
10 GEOFF CRUDGINGTON (1979-88)	326
11 CHRIS HARRISON (1975-85)	324
12 LEIGH COOPER (1979-90)	323
13 MOSES RUSSELL (1920-30)	314

14 JOHN UZZELL (1977-89)	311
15 JOHN NEWMAN (1959-68)	298
16 GORDON NISBET (1980-87)	281
17 NEIL DOUGALL (1948-59)	274
18 TOMMY TYNAN (1983-90)	262
19 GEORGE DEWS (1947-55)	257
20 WILF CARTER (1957-64)	253

<u>LEAGUE AND CUP APPEARANCES, PLYMOUTH ARGYLE PLAYERS</u>

1 KEVIN HODGES (1978-)	554
2 SAMMY BLACK (1924-38)	491
3 JOHNNY WILIAMS (1955-66)	447
4 PAT JONES (1946-58)	441
5 JOHN HORE (1964-76)	441
6 JACK LESLIE (1921-35)	400
7 FRED CRIAG (1920-30)	389
8 LEIGH COOPER (1979-90)	386
9 GEOFF CRUDGINGTON (1979-88)	385
10 GEORGE ROBERTSON (1950-64)	380
11 CHRIS HARRISON (1975-85)	380
12 BILL SHORTT (1946-56)	356
13 JOHN UZZELL (1977-89)	349
14 MOSES RUSSELL (1920-30)	339
15 GORDON NISBET (1980-87)	333
16 JOHN NEWMAN (1959-68)	328
17 TOMMY TYNAN (1983-90)	310
18 NEIL DOUGALL (1948-59)	289
19 WILF CARTER (1932-40)	274
20 GEORGE DEWS (1947-55)	271

<u>PLYMOUTH ARGYLE'S TOP TEN SCORERS (LEAGUE)</u>

	G	Pld
1 SAMMY BLACK (1924-38)	176	470
2 WILF CARTER (1957-64)	134	253
3 JACK LESLIE (1921-35)	131	383
4 TOMMY TYNAN (1983-90)	127	262
5 MAURICE TADMAN (1947-55)	108	240
6 JACK VIDLER (1928-39)	95	243
7 RAY BOWDEN (1926-33)	83	145
8 KEVIN HODGES (1978-)	78	470
9 GEORGE DEWS (1947-55)	76	257
10 JACK COCK (1924-28)	72	90

PLYMOUTH ARGYLE'S TOP TEN SCORERS (OVERALL)

1 SAMMY BLACK (1924-38)	185	491
2 WILF CARTER (1957-64)	148	274
3 TOMMY TYNAN (1983-90)	146	310
4 JACK LESLIE (1921-35)	134	400

5 MAURICE TADMAN (1947-55)	112	253
6 JACK VIDLER (1928-39)	103	257
7 RAY BOWDEN (1926-33)	87	153
8 KEVIN HODGES (1978-)	82	554
9 GEORGE DEWS (1947-55)	81	271
10 JACK COCK (1924-28)	74	92

PLYMOUTH ARGYLE PLAYERS, LEAGUE GAMES PER GOAL

1 JACK COCK (1924-28)	1.25
2 RAY BOWDEN (1926-33)	1.75
3 WILF CARTER (1957-64)	1.89
4 TOMMY TYNAN (1983-90)	2.06
5 MAURICE TADMAN (1947-55)	2.22
6 JACK VIDLER (1928-39)	2.56
7 SAMMY BLACK (1924-38)	2.67
8 JACK LESLIE (1921-35)	2.92
9 GEORGE DEWS (1947-55)	3.38
10 KEVIN HODGES (1978-)	6.03

PLYMOUTH ARGYLE PLAYERS, LEAGUE AND CUP GAMES PER GOAL

1 JACK COCK (1924-28)	1.24
2 RAY BOWDEN (1926-33)	1.76
3 WILF CARTER (1957-64)	1.89
4 TOMMY TYNAN (1983-90)	2.12
5 MAURICE TADMAN (1947-55)	2.26
6 JACK VIDLER (1928-39)	2.50
7 SAMMY BLACK (1924-38)	2.65
8 JACK LELSIE (1921-35)	2.98
9 GEORGE DEWS (1947-55)	3.35
10 KEVIN HODGES (1978-)	6.76

TRANSFER TRAIL

Nov1972: Signed professional for Liverpoool.
Oct 1975: From Liverpool to Swansea City - loan.
Nov1975: From Swansea City to Liverpool - loan over.
Sep 1976: From Liverpool to Sheffield Weednesday - £10,000.
Oct 1978: From Sheffield Wednesday to Lincoln City - £33,000.
Feb 1979: From Lincoln City to Newport County £25,000.
Aug1983: From Newport County to Plymouth Argyle £55,000.
Jul 1985: From Plymouth Argyle to Rotherham United - £25,000.
Apr 1986: From Rotherham United to Plymouth Argyle -loan.
May1986: From Plymouth Argyle to Rotherham United - loan over.
Sep 1986: From Rotherham United to Plymouth Argyle - £25,000.
May1990: From Plymouth Argyle to Torquay United - free.
Total moves: 11 (7 permenant, 2 loans and return).
Total outlay: £173,000.

ACKNOWLEDGEMENTS

DEBTS OF gratitude are owed to many people who have helped with the production of this book and without whose efforts, guidance, contributions and sustenance it would not have seen the light of day.

Thanks to: Nick Carney (and his computer), for the cover design and lay-out work which belie his tender years; Tony Carney, Chief Photographer of the Evening Herald, Plymouth, whose work - which demonstrates his considerable talent of being in exactly the right place and the right time - adorns the cover and inside pages; the Evening Herald, for kind permission to use the photographs; Mike Sampson, of the Design & Print Workshop, Plympton, for a service above the normal call of duty (and meals along the way); Colin Davison, Editor of the Western Morning News, for encouragement; Ross Reid, Sports Editor of the Western Morning News, for turning his blind eye on the odd occasion that the book took precedence over the Great Mills League results and turning his keen eye to the proof reading; Paul Stapleton and Terry Copeland, manager of Barclay's Bank, Plymouth, for advice in matters financial; the Design & Print Workshop, for all their help; Elaine, Tammy, Keeley, Jordanna and Thomas, for allowing their front room to be turned into an interview studio; the Evening Herald's photographic crew, for use of their computer; colleagues, friends and Plymouth Argyle supporters, for their freely given advice and encouragement; Sue Carney, for tea; and the person or people who have almost certainly and certainly undeservedly been overlooked in writing this epilogue.

To everyone, much thanks.